# THOSE LAMBTONS!

### A most unusual family

# THOSE LAMBTONS!

### A most unusual family

# SIR JOHN COLVILLE

## Hodder & Stoughton
### LONDON  SYDNEY  AUCKLAND  TORONTO

*British Library Cataloguing in Publication Data*
Colville, John, *1915–1987*
  Those Lambtons!: a most unusual
family.
  1. Lambton. (*Family*)
  I. Title
  942.082'092'2      CT787.L3

ISBN 0-340-42768-X

Dedicated to my wife and children whose
Lambton peculiarities are never far below
the surface.

# Contents

# Illustrations

———◆———

The photographs that appear between pages 100 and 101 are from the author's private collection.

# Acknowledgments

In writing this book I have been much indebted, first to the Queen, for allowing me access to the papers in the Royal Archives relating to Admiral of the Fleet Sir Hedworth Meux and General Sir William Lambton, and for letting me quote from the letters of Edward, Prince of Wales, to Sir William.

Apart from that important source, the letters of Sir William during the First World War were placed at my disposal by Lord Lambton and information about the sale of the Lambton collieries was provided by Lord Joicey and Mrs. Carol Wensby-Scott. Otherwise I have made little use of manuscript sources: the lives of Radical Jack, 1st Earl of Durham, and his grandson, George Lambton, have been amply researched, and for the others I have relied partly on private information and partly on personal knowledge.

As regards Radical Jack the three chapters of this book relating to him are based to some extent on the excellent biography published in 1929 by Professor Chester New of MacMaster University, Toronto – *Lord Durham, the Biography of John George Lambton*, published by Clarendon Press, Oxford, and Dawsons of Pall Mall and reissued in 1968. The Professor made a thorough examination of all the papers at Lambton Castle and in the Canadian archives. I have also made use of some social sidelights gathered from *The Diary of Jane Ellice* edited by Patricia Godsell and published in Canada by Oberon Press in 1976.

George Lambton was his own biographer, but I have been helped (except in the passages which refer to her personally) by the advice of his daughter, Professor Ann Lambton, and by Mr. Michael Seth-Smith's lucid description of the breach between Lambton and Lord Derby in his book, *A Classic Connection*, Secker & Warburg, 1983.

Lady Susan Askew has provided valuable material. Lord Lambton, Lord Home of the Hirsel and Mr. William Douglas-Home have been constructive critics of the chapters which concern them, though Lord Home complains that I have been too generous in my assessment of his career and personality. With that I do not agree.

Finally I am indebted to Sally Wilson who has painstakingly deciphered and typed my pencilled manuscript.

JOHN COLVILLE
1987

# Those Lambtons!

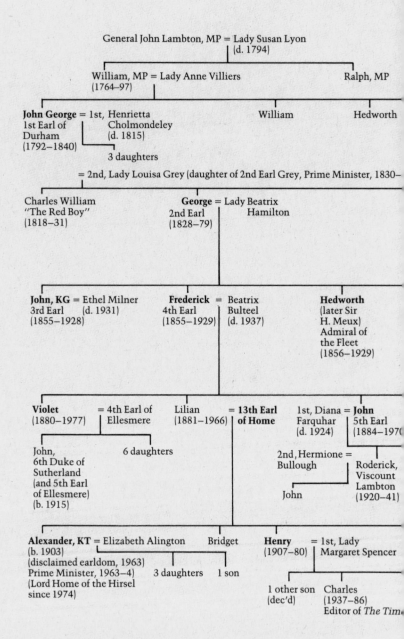

General John Lambton, MP = Lady Susan Lyon (d. 1794)

William, MP = Lady Anne Villiers (1764–97)

Ralph, MP

John George = 1st, Henrietta
1st Earl of      Cholmondeley
Durham           (d. 1815)
(1792–1840)

William

Hedworth

3 daughters

= 2nd, Lady Louisa Grey (daughter of 2nd Earl Grey, Prime Minister, 1830–

Charles William
"The Red Boy"
(1818–31)

George = Lady Beatrix
2nd Earl     Hamilton
(1828–79)

John, KG = Ethel Milner
3rd Earl      (d. 1931)
(1855–1928)

Frederick = Beatrix
4th Earl      Bulteel
(1855–1929)  (d. 1937)

Hedworth
(later Sir
H. Meux)
Admiral of
the Fleet
(1856–1929)

Violet         = 4th Earl of
(1880–1977)   | Ellesmere

Lilian
(1881–1966)

= 13th Earl
| of Home

1st, Diana = John
Farquhar    5th Earl
(d. 1924)   (1884–197(

John,
6th Duke of
Sutherland
(and 5th Earl
of Ellesmere)
(b. 1915)

6 daughters

2nd, Hermione =
Bullough

John

Roderick,
Viscount
Lambton
(1920–41)

Alexander, KT = Elizabeth Alington
(b. 1903)
(disclaimed earldom, 1963)
Prime Minister, 1963–4)
(Lord Home of the Hirsel
since 1974)

Bridget

3 daughters   1 son

Henry        = 1st, Lady
(1907–80)   | Margaret Spencer

1 other son    Charles
(dec'd)        (1937–86)
               Editor of The Tim

# A SELECTIVE FAMILY TREE OF THE LAMBTONS

(names in bold are
substantially mentioned
in the text)

Frances

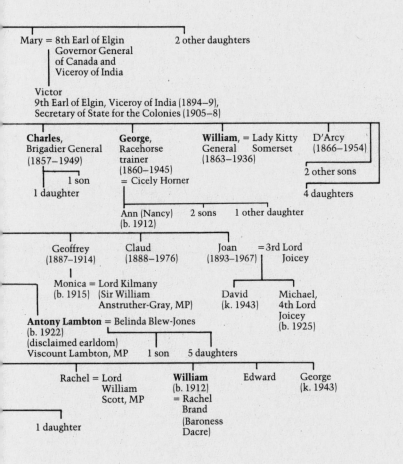

Mary = 8th Earl of Elgin     2 other daughters
Governor General
of Canada and
Viceroy of India

Victor
9th Earl of Elgin, Viceroy of India (1894–9),
Secretary of State for the Colonies (1905–8)

**Charles**,    **George**,    **William**, = Lady Kitty    D'Arcy
Brigadier General   Racehorse    General    Somerset    (1866–1954)
(1857–1949)    trainer     (1863–1936)
     (1860–1945)              2 other sons
1 son    = Cicely Horner
1 daughter                        4 daughters

Ann (Nancy)    2 sons    1 other daughter
(b. 1912)

Geoffrey    Claud    Joan    = 3rd Lord
(1887–1914)    (1888–1976)    (1893–1967)    Joicey

Monica = Lord Kilmany        David    Michael,
(b. 1915)   (Sir William      (k. 1943)    4th Lord
         Anstruther-Gray, MP)          Joicey

**Antony Lambton** = Belinda Blew-Jones       (b. 1925)
(b. 1922)
(disclaimed earldom)
Viscount Lambton, MP    1 son    5 daughters

Rachel = Lord    **William**    Edward    George
       William    (b. 1912)               (k. 1943)
       Scott, MP    = Rachel
               Brand
1 daughter           (Baroness
                 Dacre)

# Prologue

During the last two hundred years the Lambton family has displayed characteristics of a somewhat unusual kind, handed down from generation to generation and sometimes erupting like geysers in New Zealand. One or two of them were famous in their day, but have long been forgotten. They have nearly all had a vivid streak of eccentricity and many have combined that with ability. Characteristics common to all have been an inclination both to say and to do the unexpected, together with a total indifference to fashion and convention occasionally bordering on disdain.

There is an unresolved altercation between those who believe that it is heredity which predominates and those convinced it is primarily environment and upbringing which mould personality. I have no doubt that in some families renowned in the history of these islands a strain introduced by an ancestor has long persisted. Human beings cannot be bred as predictably as race-horses, but it is wrong not to give weight to the influence of ancestry, however much cross-breeding may adulterate the original strain.

Some representatives of the great families which ruled Britain in the eighteenth and nineteenth centuries have shown brilliance, the Russells, Cecils, Stanleys and Churchills being outstanding examples. Others have been notable for their eccentricity, a characteristic sometimes accompanied by intelligence and sometimes closer to insanity.

The intelligent eccentrics included the celebrated Harty-Tarty, 8th Duke of Devonshire, whose influence was far-reaching, but who made a habit of sleeping on the governmental front bench until, awoken from his slumbers by some Opposition speaker, he would rise to his feet and give a devastating reply to a speech of which he had probably heard about a fragment. He seldom spoke at meetings of the Cabinet, but when he did it was usually just to say "Far better not", which must often have been sound advice.

In writing *Melbourne*, Lord David Cecil discovered that Lord Althorp, Leader of the House of Commons in the Reform Bill Parliament, and himself a dedicated reformer, once replied to an opponent who raised an awkward point in the House that he had some facts with which he felt sure he could answer it but had temporarily forgotten them. As he was held in great affection on both sides of the House this reply was deemed entirely satisfactory.

A. J. Balfour, nephew of the Prime Minister, Lord Salisbury, and his eventual successor, used to read the printed copies of secret Foreign Office despatches in the train and then absent-mindedly discard them out of the window on to the railway line. However, the speed with which his brain worked was still more remarkable than his absent-mindedness. There can never have been a quicker repartee than when somebody asserted sugar to be the only word in the English language beginning with an S but pronounced with SH. "Are you sure?" said Balfour.

There were many great landowners, in addition to the Lambtons, who cared nothing for popularity or for the opinion of their friends and neighbours. Thus the 3rd Lord Crewe, a conscientious landlord, obliged the Grand Junction Railway Company to divert its London to Manchester line round his estate rather than allow a new-fangled form of transport to disturb his broad Cheshire acres. By way of revenge the company bought the village of Church Coppenhall, just outside his demesne, turned it into a railway town and, to his indignation, changed its name to Crewe.

Still odder was the 5th Duke of Portland who built a vast underground complex at Welbeck including a road along which he could drive unseen to the railway station at Worksop. He presented each of his army of workers with a donkey to ride and an umbrella and was, it seems, a good landlord, much respected locally. His sister, Lady Howard de Walden, left her personal maid, who had served her for years, nothing but a pair of stays in her will, declaring that the faithful servant's figure had become deplorable. Lord Rothschild, much esteemed as a scientist, had a coach drawn by four zebras.

The Cecil family almost invariably flouted convention, but they may have realised they had gone a bit too far when Lord Salisbury, at the time both Prime Minister and Foreign Secretary, was refused entry to the Monte Carlo Casino because he was so shabbily dressed. One of his sons, Lord William Cecil, Bishop of Exeter, was known both for his sanctity and for his vagueness. He traversed his diocese on a bicycle. It broke down one day and a young man stopped to help him repair it. When the job was done, the Bishop said, "Do you remember which way I was going?"

"That way, My Lord."

"Ah, that means I have had luncheon."

The 15th Earl of Derby was seen, on three successive days, on the race-course at Newmarket, translating Homer's *Iliad* into elegant English verse, and speaking in Parliament as Prime Minister. Some thought it odd that Lord Halifax's deep religious devotion, Fellowship of All Souls and high offices of state as Viceroy of India, Foreign Secretary and Ambassador in Washington seldom interrupted his addiction to fox-hunting. Lord Waterford, disliking his local parson, stealthily contrived to have his walking shoes impregnated with aniseed and then hunted the reverend gentleman across country with bloodhounds. The Duchess of Somerset, Queen of Beauty at the Eglinton Tournament, the flamboyant, mock-mediaeval jamboree in Renfrewshire, kept a carving knife in her carriage to ward off highwaymen, even though the last of those villains had been hanged a full hundred years before. Lord Sefton, when invited to stay at Windsor Castle, took his own wine with him, and Lord Lonsdale drank brandy at breakfast.

These are but a few examples of noble eccentricity; but strangely enough such curious habits do not seem to have affected the efficiency or beneficence of most of their exponents. The majority had been brought up to care dutifully for the welfare of their tenants and dependants, even though their younger children were usually neglected financially.

The Lambtons were frequently eccentric and were not in the least interested in the effect their words or actions made on others. They were, however, public-spirited and disposed, both by birth and tradition, to serve their country in one way or another. I have attempted to describe a succession of them from the end of the eighteenth century, when injections of Lyon and Villiers blood had stimulating results. The senior branch of the present-day Lambtons is descended twice over from that patient, good-natured, but at the same time resolute statesman, Charles, Earl Grey, who transformed the Whigs into Liberals and presided over the Government which enacted the great Reform Bill of 1832.

I have wandered into an account of collaterals in the persons of various Douglas-Homes whose mother, Lilian, was a daughter of the 4th Earl of Durham. I have not included the children of her sister, Violet Ellesmere, eccentric though she could sometimes be, partly because I am married to one of them and do not want to get into trouble, and partly because, though inheriting the family good looks and fine features, they have in the main proved reputable and reasonably uncomplicated; nor have they been remotely concerned with politics or academic achievement. The same is true of Joan Joicey's surviving son, Michael.

If it be true that "lives of great men all remind us we can make our lives sublime," only a few of them, mainly writers, poets, artists, philosophers and composers, do in fact leave footprints in the sands of time; and some of those footprints grow faint as the years pass by. Statesmen, philanthropists, reformers and even inventors (unless they attach their names to an enduring product) tend to be forgotten by all but historians a generation or so after their death.

Thus the nineteenth-century giants who, apart from the artists, musicians and writers, are still remembered at the end of the twentieth century are a scanty band: Napoleon, Queen Victoria, Bismarck, Wellington, Nelson, Abraham Lincoln and a few others. Even Gladstone and Disraeli, Peel, Palmerston and Canning, are names unfamiliar beyond the shores of the British Isles. Shelley wrote savagely (and unfairly) of Castlereagh: Shelley's name is still widely known, even if much of his poetry is no longer widely read, but Castlereagh's is not.

A successor to the omniscient school-boy, to whom Macaulay was wont to attribute the most precocious intelligence, would be hard put to it nowadays to recall such once-famous names as Talleyrand and Thiers, Cavour and Garibaldi. He would have to be exceptionally erudite to have heard of John George, 1st Earl of Durham, whose name was a household word in Britain and in Canada a hundred and fifty years ago.

# Part One

# 1

# Radical Jack

The Lambtons have been great landowners in County Durham for at least eight hundred years. They fought with gallantry in the Crusades, on Flodden Field and at Marston Moor; but it was not till the second half of the eighteenth century that they were known beyond the confines of their own county. Coal and matrimony then combined to give them fame and fortune. Rich seams of coal lay beneath their land and its exploitation steadily enlarged the family income.

In 1763, General John Lambton married Lady Susan Lyon, daughter of the Earl of Strathmore, a lady at once clever and forceful. The General represented Durham in six successive parliaments but refused an earldom offered to him by Lord Chatham, of whom he disapproved. His son, William, followed in his parliamentary footsteps. Such were his

27

advanced political views that there was no likelihood of
William Pitt, the Younger, renewing his father's offer.

Unlike the General, who was an unambitious politician,
William became a dedicated protagonist of parliamentary
reform. With his friends from Trinity College, Cambridge,
Charles Grey and Samuel Whitbread, he nailed his flag to
the mast of Charles James Fox's jolly, but not very seaworthy
ship. The crew formed the "Society of the Friends of the
People", with the stated object of restoring freedom of election and a more equal representation of the people in Parliament; and they also fought valiantly, though unavailingly,
to defeat the suspension of *habeas corpus* imposed by an
Administration fearful that the French revolutionary infec-
tion might cross the Channel. William married Lady Anne
Villiers, whose father, the 4th Earl of Jersey, had been a Lord
of the Admiralty and Lord Chamberlain to King George III.
The Villiers were an intelligent family and though Lady
Anne herself was extravagant and inclined to be feckless,
she contributed genes of some significance to her children.

In 1797 William, by then highly regarded both in the
north of England and at Westminster, died of consumption
when he was only thirty-three. His eldest son, John George,
thus succeeded to a vast estate and fortune at the age of five.

Lady Anne soon married again and departed from Lambton
Castle, which her husband had started to build high above
the River Wear in the new Gothic revival fashion. There it still
stands, gaunt and empty but maintained in good order and
bordered by well-mown lawns, commanding a magnificent
view of the large park and screened from the surrounding
conurbations. John George and one of his brothers, Hedworth, were sent away to a school at Clifton, near Bristol, run
by a Dr. Beddoes who had been removed from the Chair of
Chemistry at Oxford because of his sympathy with the
French Revolution. The good doctor was an excellent teacher
with advanced liberal convictions who taught the boys phys-
ics, chemistry, French and elementary economics in addition
to the Latin and Greek which were the sole curriculum in
most schools. Moreover, Mrs. Beddoes was a sister of the

novelist Maria Edgeworth and in the literary circle which she cultivated the boys met both Coleridge and Southey. Under Dr. Beddoes' tuition John George learned not only to speak clearly but also – then as now most important – to use an economy of words both in speech and writing.

At thirteen he went to Eton for three years. There he was only noted for his debating "support of popular rather than oligarchical principles of Government", a thesis unlikely to win applause in a Tory school (the Whigs tended to send their sons to Harrow), but one for which his father's example, combined with Dr. Beddoes' teaching, was doubtless responsible. Though his political instincts were liberal, his temperament was autocratic. He declined to go to a university but demanded the purchase of a Cornet's commission in the army. He got his way, as he almost always did, but after two years in the Tenth Light Dragoons and the purchase of a Lieutenancy, he sold his commission and fell in love.

The object of his affection was the beautiful Henrietta Cholmondeley, illegitimate daughter of Lord Cholmondeley and a French actress. The word actress was probably a euphemism. Henrietta should, of course, have borne her mother's surname, but that was French and the Cheshire neighbours would have been scandalised. As for John George, he was only nineteen and he had problems with his guardians. So he eloped with Henrietta, who was also under age, to Gretna Green and married her at the smithy on January 1st, 1812. To his pleasant surprise the Cholmondeleys approved the run-away match, perhaps because Henrietta was more attractive than her legitimate half-sister, and a few weeks later the happy couple were solemnly remarried in the Cholmondeleys' parish church, the new Mrs. Lambton reverting to her assumed maiden name for the ceremony.

As soon as he was twenty-one, in 1813, John George rudely required his uncle and former guardian, Ralph Lambton, to vacate his seat as Member for the City of Durham, since two Lambton M.P.s in Durham might be regarded as excessive. He himself was then elected M.P. for the County. Thenceforward politics were his obsession, only varied by a lively

interest in racing, unceasing care for his family and the conscientious performance of his duties as land and coal owner.
Luckily, as he was away from home for long periods, he acquired an exceptionally able, honest and philanthropic agent.

There are three biographies of "Radical Jack", as he was
later almost universally known, and they are based on vol-
uminous family papers. To epitomise them in detail would
lead to an accusation of plagiarism; but as John George
Lambton, 1st Earl of Durham, made a major contribution,
perhaps indeed the greatest, to two vitally important developments in the nineteenth century, the account of his
achievements bears repetition. It is, indeed, surprising that
this man whose name was on everybody's lips in the 1830s,
whose presence attracted enormous crowds of enthusiastic
supporters, should towards the end of the twentieth century
be remembered only by a few historians and scarcely mentioned in the history books used by the present generation
in Britain, even if in Canada his fame still persists. He was
the subject of abuse by Tory diarists such as Greville and
Croker; and that amusing but most spiteful of sneak-guests,
Creevey, helped to blacken his name. Even the level-headed
Lord David Cecil has, in his adulation of Lord Melbourne,
failed to give Radical Jack the credit that is his due.

His notoriety among his contemporaries was combined
with unpopularity among those of his own station in life.
That was only partly his own fault. Spoilt as a child, remark-
ably good-looking, rich beyond the dreams of avarice, fiery
in his outbursts of temper and a curious blend of arrogance
and modesty, he was pursued by two malignant Furies.

One was persistent family bereavement. The bewitching
Henrietta died of consumption after three years of marriage.
He then married Lady Louisa Grey, daughter of his father's
friend, Charles, Earl Grey, who was later the Whig Prime
Minister at the time of the Reform Bill. Although he had been
christened John George, Louisa always called him Lambton,
as did her father. Their elder son, Charles, the subject of
Lawrence's famous portrait, "Master Lambton" or "The Red
Boy", who was the light in his parents' eyes, died of

30

consumption at the age of thirteen. He was followed within the next four years by Lambton's mother and all three of his deeply loved daughters by Henrietta Cholmondeley. Consumption, which eventually carried off Lambton himself, was the great killer of those times. Its dread tentacles seized all the children by his first marriage of Lambton's contemporary, Lord Aberdeen, and wrought havoc to the families of both the rich and the poor throughout the first half of the nineteenth century.

The second malignant Fury was Lambton's own health. When he was a boy Dr. Beddoes, a skilled medical practitioner as well as an eminent scientist, detected a threat of consumption; and from his early twenties until his death he was laid low at frequent intervals by devastating pains in his head so that he was often obliged to lie for days on end in a darkened room. It may have been migraine; it may have been neuralgia. Probably it was both, but a cure was beyond the skill of contemporary doctors, as indeed it might be today. Laudanum was the only defence against those devastating attacks which almost invariably struck him down at times of emotional stress. Perhaps, like many great men, he was basically a manic depressive.

During the 1820s, in the intervals of his attendance at the House of Commons, he devoted much thought to the management of his lands and collieries. A great deal of money was expended on new machinery and on drainage in the pits. He also spent £90,000 on completing Lambton Castle and lighting it with gas, a remarkable innovation which stemmed from his constant interest in the progress of the Industrial Revolution. He was proud of his position and of his wealth, driving out in splendid carriages drawn by grey horses and attended by outriders as if he were a royal prince. He saw no inconsistency between personal splendour and devotion to political democracy; but he did attend diligently to the needs of the miners in his collieries.

The life of a coal miner was dismal and dangerous. Naked lights and pockets of gas caused frequent explosions below ground and there were many disasters. Lambton became vice-president of the Society for the Prevention of Accidents in Coal Mines and he corresponded with Humphry Davy, who had been an usher in Dr. Beddoes' school at Clifton and by 1815 had been recognised as a scientist of repute. Davy visited the Lambton collieries and in 1816 produced the safety lamp which was to save countless lives in the mines. It was tried out in one of Lambton's pits, and he descended the shaft to witness the experiment.

With trade unions declared illegal by the drastic Combination Acts, miners were still wretchedly paid, bound by contracts they could not renounce and forced to work a ten-hour day below ground. Boys, who had to do the clearing up, worked for twelve hours. It is not surprising that, with the repeal of the Combination Acts in 1825, miners at once formed themselves into unions. Pit strikes began in 1831 throughout the counties of Durham and Northumberland; but the Lambton miners continued to work despite dire threats from the trade unionists in neighbouring coal fields. Their decision was mainly due to the qualities of the excellent agent, Henry Morton, whom the miners both respected and liked; but Lambton himself was zealous in maintaining good relations. In 1833, while he was in the Cabinet, he found time to establish with Henry Morton the Lambton Collieries Association. This scheme, largely financed out of his own pocket, provided accident insurance and a rudimentary pension scheme. On the first anniversary of its establishment he invited the fifty miners forming its Committee of Management to a dinner at the Castle. He spoke hotly against the trade unions, whose leaders he believed to be primarily interested in feathering their own nests, but declared that he had instructed his own agents to create schools for the miners' children and libraries for the old people. He really did care for those who worked for him and gave close attention to their wages and working conditions. They repaid his paternalism with unswerving loyalty and, indeed, affection. Of the fifty thousand people who took part in his funeral procession by no means the least conspicuous were the long lines of colliery workers.

He was, like his mother, recklessly extravagant, but also notably generous. He could afford to be. In a normal year, depending on the price of coal, his income was plus or minus £80,000 which was, in purchasing power, the equivalent of more than £2 million a year tax free in the 1980s. He told his future sister-in-law, Maria Copley, that he considered £40,000 a year a moderate income, "such a one as a man might jog on with". Unfortunately he said this in the hearing of Thomas Creevey, the prime gossip, and he was thenceforward known as "Jogalong Durham" by those who did not call him Radical Jack. Creevey himself always referred to him as King Jog.

He loved display and revelled in ceremony, combining radical and traditionalist sentiments to an extent rare even among the great Whig families. He longed for the peerage his grandfather had declined, but when in 1828 the Prime Minister, Lord Goderich, put his name forward for a barony, he accepted it with loudly expressed disappointment. This was not because it meant leaving the Commons for the Lords (who were, in the event, the more important of the two Houses in his future political career); but having been, as he proudly boasted, the first Commoner in England, he now became the junior baron, albeit, apart from royal dukes, the youngest peer ever created. He chose the title of Lord Durham, but had to wait for the earldom he desired until his retirement from the Cabinet in 1834.

In his early years he hunted and bought an expensive pack of hounds; he liked shooting; he played cricket well; but racing became his principal, though temporary, diversion. He began to own race-horses after Henrietta died and just before he married Louisa. After four totally unsuccessful seasons he had frequent successes at Doncaster, York and Newmarket, though his horse *Borodino* was defeated in the St. Leger. However, when he bought a horse called *Cedric* which had won the Derby and never been beaten, it was a failure and *Cedric* was retired after one disastrous race in the Lambton colours. Shortly afterwards he sold his racing stable and also abandoned a course he had laid out for friends and neighbours in the park at Lambton. He had too many other fish to fry.

He encouraged and partly financed an attempt to establish a colony in New Zealand. Britain's claim to those distant islands had been accepted by the Congress of Vienna in 1814, but there had been no colonisation. However, with Lambton's enthusiastic sponsorship two ships, the *Lambton* and the *Isabella*, filled with expectant settlers, sailed for the South Pacific in 1825. On arrival the adventurous pioneers were discouraged "by the number and threatening demonstrations of the aborigines", and so they changed course for New South Wales, preferring convicts to Maoris. New Zealand had to wait.

Politics were increasingly exciting. Lambton had marked his claim to a parliamentary audience as early as May 1814 with a maiden speech deploring the transfer of Norway to the Swedish Crown as a reward to Bernadotte for having betrayed Napoleon. Shortly afterwards he protested in the House against the apparently unscrupulous, if eventually sensible, bestowal of Genoa and the Genoese on the King of Sardinia. Then, when the Dukes of Clarence and Kent deserted their mistresses and rushed into matrimony with indecent speed on the death of Princess Charlotte, the Prince Regent's only child, Lambton took it on himself to oppose special matrimonial grants. The Duke of Clarence must have noted his action, unsuccessful though it was, and it may perhaps be that the distaste he then felt for Lambton accounts for the hostility he later showed when he became King William IV. Lambton was not only scrupulously honest, but he believed firmly in fidelity, if only to long-established mistresses, and he had no sympathy for arranged marriages. The Duke of Clarence did, after all, have ten illegitimate but well-cosseted children by the amiable actress, Mrs. Jordan. His legitimate marriage was childless, but his brother, the Duke of Kent, contrived to sire a daughter and heir to the throne, the Princess Victoria.

In 1819, after a successful foray in a Westminster by-election to support Lord Melbourne's brother, Charles Lamb, Lambton spoke eloquently at Durham and Sunderland in denouncing the barbarism of the yeomanry at the Peterloo massacre and the conduct of the Government thereafter.

The Durham clergy, spurred on by the bigoted and exceptionally unattractive Prebendary Phillpotts, later Bishop
of Exeter, opposed him; but he outwitted them and even
succeeded in seizing the chair at a meeting they had arranged
for the purpose of attacking him.

The Government brought in their stringent and dictatorial
Six Acts, forbidding public meetings and seditious publications. Lambton spoke ardently against these tyrannical
measures. He did more. He rose in an astonished House and
gave notice of a motion for radical parliamentary reform as
the sole remedy for popular discontent. Before he could proceed, George III died, and in those days a parliamentary dissolution automatically followed a demise of the Crown.
Lambton, now considered a dangerous revolutionary, was opposed at Durham in the ensuing General Election by the
Tory Chief Whip, energetically supported by Prebendary
Phillpotts. He addressed electors in the remotest villages,
suggested that a Bishop Rampant should be added to his opponent's coat of arms and fearlessly advocated household suffrage, shorter parliaments, the abolition of rotten boroughs
and other reforms. The election cost him £30,000, but he won
comfortably with the Tory Chief Whip at the bottom of the
poll. Phillpotts, like New Zealand, had to bide his time.

Encouraged by this success, Lambton introduced his motion
for parliamentary reform in April 1821. It was a bold venture
for a twenty-nine-year-old Member. His proposals were by and
large those that eventually prevailed in 1832 when the great
Reform Bill was passed, though in 1821 he also advocated
household suffrage, equal electoral districts, triennial parliaments, the payment of Members and secret ballots. At present,
he declared, the great majority of Members were returned
"without the remotest shadow of popular delegation".

The motion was seconded by Samuel Whitbread and might
well have attracted more support than the Government
would have wished. However, by a cunning ruse George
Canning contrived to divide the House, after an intervening
debate on the army estimates, when Lambton and his supporters were having dinner. So the motion was easily

defeated by a hundred of the Government's tame followers who had been persuaded to forgo their meal.

A few years later Lambton fought a duel. His opponent was one T. W. Beaumont who had been the Whig Member of Parliament for Northumberland, but had announced his intention of not standing again at the General Election of 1826. Lambton's father-in-law, Lord Grey, thought his son, Lord Howick, should stand for election. For some reason this annoyed Beaumont who decided that he would after all present himself once again. Howick was young and an inexperienced speaker. Therefore Lambton, leaving his own county of Durham and accompanied by both Lady Louisa and an orchestra, crossed the Tyne into Northumberland and made eloquent speeches on Howick's behalf. Beaumont was furious, considering that Lambton was trespassing on Northumbrian soil.

At an election meeting in Alnwick, where all four candidates for the seat made speeches, Beaumont accused Lambton of having prompted Howick throughout his speech. Lambton denied it, whereupon Beaumont called him a liar and when Lambton stood up to address the crowd, Beaumont's hired band began to play in order to drown his words, as did the band of one of the other candidates. Electioneering in those days was highly orchestral. Lambton challenged Beaumont to a duel for having called him a liar.

Duelling, not finally discontinued till the 1840s, was illegal even in 1826, though it was socially and above all militarily acceptable. Canning had fought Castlereagh, and as late as 1829 the Duke of Wellington fought the Earl of Winchilsea, all without the slightest damage to their opponents. However, there were risks of an unpleasant accident, for killing an opponent in a duel was murder. In George III's reign over ninety successful duellists were sentenced to death, though only two were actually executed.

Lambton's challenge to Beaumont promised a spectacle for local enjoyment, but the magistrates heard what was afoot and took all possible steps to prevent it. So did Lord Grey who rode alone on horseback from Howick to Alnwick moor only to find that the authorities had arrived at the moor and forestalled the duellists. Both the crowds of expectant spectators and the authorities were finally outwitted and Lambton met Beaumont on Bamburgh Sands. They exchanged shots. Both missed, as was usually the case on such occasions, and honour was felt to be satisfied. Few things were more ridiculous than nineteenth-century political duels, though angry officers in the army did sometimes damage each other seriously and were thereafter cashiered.

When the long-lasting Tory Prime Minister, Lord Liverpool, retired in 1827, there was a brief Administration under Canning, somewhat more Liberal than his predecessor and supported by a section of both the Whigs and Tories. But Canning died within a few months and after a brief spell under Lord Goderich the Government fell into the hands of the staunchly anti-Reformist Duke of Wellington. Wellington was obliged to concede Catholic emancipation, which Lambton, now Lord Durham, strongly supported, though he had opposed it in 1825 (to the indignation of his parliamentary associates) not because he objected to the principle, but because the measure was to be combined with the disfranchisement of the Irish forty-shilling freeholders.

George IV's brother, the Duke of York, heir to the throne, had also opposed Catholic emancipation in 1825. Rising in the House of Lords he prophesied that if Roman Catholics were emancipated there would soon be no King in England, Parliament would be destroyed and Mass would be celebrated in Westminster Abbey. The Lords threw out the Bill. The Duke of York was, as it happened, right on two counts: by the end of 1837 there was no King, for Queen Victoria sat on the throne, and the old Houses of Parliament had been burned to the ground; but Westminster Abbey remained unshakeably Anglican. The measure was finally accepted by Parliament two years after the Duke of York died, and, amongst others, the Duke of Norfolk, Earl Marshal of England, was allowed to take his seat in the House of Lords. He did so with approval by Durham who was no Protestant zealot. It is fortunate that the Grand Old Duke of York did not outlive his brother and become King Frederick the First.

Had he done so, there would assuredly have been no Reform Bill and there might well have been a revolution.

There was not long to wait. The Canningites moved further away from the main body of the Tories and in November 1830 the Duke of Wellington made an inept speech in the Lords saying that he would resist any measure of parliamentary reform whatever. The country seethed with rage, and political unions, formed with huge popular support in Birmingham and Manchester, Sheffield and Hull, held mass demonstrations. They hailed Durham as their champion.

King George IV had died in the summer of 1830, and a General Election was pending. Liberal passions were inflamed by a rising in Poland and by the revolution in France which ousted the last of the Bourbons. In England, too, the country seemed to be on the edge of a precipice. There had been outbreaks of savage violence, punished by executions and large-scale deportations to the Australian convict settlements, for which the ultimate responsibility lay with Lord Melbourne, a Whig incongruously serving as Home Secretary in Wellington's Administration.

Fortunately Wellington's intransigent Government was defeated in the House of Commons in November, the Canningites voting with the Whigs. The new King, William IV, sent for Lord Grey, Durham's much-loved father-in-law, to form a Whig Government and propose a measure of parliamentary reform.

Edmund Burke said in exoneration of Charles Townshend, Chancellor of the Exchequer in Lord Chatham's Administration and one of the guiltier parties in the events leading up to the revolt of the American colonies: "He had no passions which were not owing to a noble cause; to an ardent, generous, perhaps an immoderate passion for fame; a passion which is the instinct of all great souls." Fifty years after Townshend died, Burke's words might equally have been applied to Lambton whose passion for parliamentary reform was "owing to a noble cause". The family motto was, and is, *Le Jour Viendra*. In 1831 it did.

# 2

# The Reform Bill

King William IV sent for the Whigs to pacify the country by converting the long-lasting mirage of parliamentary reform into reality, but the question was how far they would have to go. The very word democracy was anathema to the King and to most of the leading politicians, including the Whigs themselves. They equated it with anarchy and mob rule. An exception was Durham who with the strident support of the extreme Radicals, and the cooperation of a brilliant lawyer, Henry Brougham, wished to go a long way on the road to popular government. He much disliked trade unions and potential revolutionaries. His belief in the established order, King, Church and Parliament, was unshakeable; but he believed, with equal passion, that these venerable institutions must modernise themselves in keeping with the age introduced by the Industrial Revolution.

In November 1830 the new Prime Minister, Lord Grey, busy with the formation of his Government, asked his son-in-law to prepare a Reform Bill. To do so Durham was appointed Lord Privy Seal, with a seat in the Cabinet but no departmental duties to take his mind off the task. He accepted with alacrity, though in other circumstances he would have preferred the Foreign Office. That went to Lord Palmerston.

Durham chaired a committee of ministers: Lord John Russell, Sir James Graham of Netherby and his wife Louisa's uncle, the sensible Lord Duncannon, were the other members. They met secretly every day at Durham's house in Cleveland Row and hammered out the draft of a bill. He provided the overall inspiration, but it was Lord John Russell, small of stature, scholarly, pedantic, but assiduous in every task he shouldered, who did most of the detailed work and recommended which rotten boroughs were to be wholly or partly disfranchised. So secret were their deliberations that no outsiders were admitted and only a few intimate colleagues, such as Lord Althorp, Leader of the House of Commons, were consulted. Durham acted as secretary as well as chairman: Louisa and her eldest daughter, Mary, did the necessary copying. There were no moles, not even Creevey.

Needless to say Durham, who was impetuous and had never recognised the wisdom of the Latin tag *festina lente* – hasten slowly – wanted to include more than his colleagues judged Parliament could be induced to accept. He insisted on provisions for triennial parliaments and secret ballots. Without the latter, which in the event were not introduced till 1872, he saw that corruption could not be eliminated from parliamentary elections. There were arguments in the committee on this score, but Durham prevailed.

All the members of the committee worked hard and they completed in two hectic months the draft of what seemed to them a revolutionary change in British politics, though in fact it took four more Reform Bills to change at all noticeably the composition of the House of Commons.

40

Much of the credit for the first of those Bills, which paved the way for the others, must be given to Lord John Russell; but the final draft did not differ greatly from the Bill Durham had daringly laid before an unreceptive House of Commons in 1821. Throughout the subsequent campaign he and Russell were ardently supported by Althorp and by the new Lord Chancellor, Brougham.

Three years later, when Durham and Russell wished to disprove Brougham's claim to have been the principal promoter of the Reform Bill, they agreed to make statements in their respective Houses disclosing what had been argued and finally agreed by the committee and by the Cabinet. Lord Melbourne, by then Prime Minister, wrote to the King, who had at first approved this proposal: "If the arguments in Cabinet are no longer to be protected by an impenetrable veil of secrecy, there will be no place left on the public councils for the free investigations of truth and the unshackled exercise of understanding."

By this somewhat strange phraseology he meant that the deliberations of the Cabinet must remain confidential if Ministers are to speak their minds freely. It is a pity that some Cabinet Ministers in the last half of the twentieth century paid no attention to Melbourne's words or, indeed, to their oaths as Privy Councillors.

The committee of four presented the draft Bill to Lord Grey on January 14th, 1831. Durham had agreed to substitute five years for three as the life of a parliament, but he was passionately insistent on the secret ballot. The draft was accompanied by a covering letter which each had signed, stating that they believed the Bill's adoption would be the surest and "most effectual check to that restless spirit of innovation, which, founding its open claims to public support on the impossibility and hopelessness of obtaining any redress of acknowledged abuses, aims in secret at nothing less than the overthrow of all our institutions and even of the throne itself".

A few days later the proposals were submitted to the full Cabinet. Durham, exhausted by his efforts and distraught by the news that his treasured son Charles was incurably ill, collapsed and lay in a darkened room in Cleveland Row unable to attend meetings. In his absence the Cabinet threw out the secret ballot proposal. Durham felt he had been betrayed; but he had not been at the Cabinet to argue the case, which he might well have done effectively.

The King was in Brighton, viewing with the astonishment and dislike of a bluff naval officer his late brother's oriental extravagances at the Pavilion. Grey went there to seek royal approval for the submission of the Bill to Parliament. King William disliked change on principle, but he was impressed by the committee's covering letter about the threat of revolution and gave his consent. "If the King is with us, the battle is won," wrote Sir James Graham; but it was far from so being. However, the powerful political unions at Birmingham and elsewhere, whose leaders were meritoriously opposed to violence, thought it well to watch events and to keep their powder dry.

On March 1st, 1831, Lord John Russell rose in the House of Commons to introduce the Bill. The debate lasted a week; day by day there was increasing pressure in support of it from outside the House. This was to be the Great Charter of the middle classes, of those who paid £10 in rates, and they eagerly looked forward to crowding through a door where entry had hitherto been largely reserved for the ruling class. On its second reading, amid scenes of turbulent excitement in the lobbies, the Bill was approved by 302 votes to 301. Popular turmoil temporarily subsided, but the Government, in search of a working majority to carry the Bill through the Committee stage, asked for a Dissolution. The King somewhat reluctantly granted it after the Government had been narrowly defeated in opposing a motion not to reduce the total number of Members.

The Lords then bared their noble teeth. Lord Wharncliffe gave notice on March 21st that he would introduce on the morrow a motion praying the King not to use his prerogative of Dissolution, a motion which it would have been difficult for the King to disregard. The subsequent events were so melodramatic as to come close to farce. Their happy outcome may well have staved off revolutionary violence, for although the mob were not to share in the proposed middle-class bonanza they were fierce supporters of the Bill. It was therefore vital to forestall Lord Wharncliffe and for that purpose the King must go down to Parliament in person. Commissioners authorised to act on his behalf, as is normal in a Dissolution, could be kept waiting while Wharncliffe's motion was proposed and undoubtedly approved by a majority of his fellow peers without debate. The King, however, could not be kept waiting.

William IV summoned a meeting of the Privy Council for noon on March 22nd. The House of Lords was to meet at 2 p.m., and by the time the King, who resented Lord Wharncliffe's impudence, had agreed to dissolve Parliament in person, it was almost one o'clock. Brougham had already, without due authority, summoned an escort from the Horse Guards to proceed to St. James's Palace; Grey was entrusted with the Sword of State and Durham was invited to carry the Cap of Maintenance. Although the King had not yet been crowned, that symbol of majesty was fetched in haste from the Tower and reached the House of Lords in a hackney cab. Durham found the Master of the Horse, Lord Albemarle, having a late breakfast and told him he must have the royal carriages made ready instantly. When Durham objected to his first finishing his breakfast, Albemarle said: "Lord bless me! Is there a revolution?" "Not at the moment," replied Durham, "but there will be if you wait to finish your breakfast."

It was just in time. The guns from the Tower resounded down the Thames to announce the King's approach. Sir Robert Peel[1] attempted to ignore Black Rod knocking on the door to summon the faithful Commons. Lord Wharncliffe was already on his feet in the Lords, but after an interruption from the Woolsack Lord Mansfield began to make a long-winded speech, thus inadvertently gagging Wharncliffe. While Wharncliffe was protesting, the doors swung open, Durham and Grey bearing the Cap of Mainten-

[1] Sir Robert Peel, M.P., Leader in the House of Commons of the Conservative Party (first so called in 1831) and future Prime Minister.

ance and the Sword of State were seen advancing, and then the King entered the House, quite improperly wearing the Crown, not yet altered to fit his head which was smaller than George IV's. With dignity he dissolved a by no means dignified Parliament.

After the ensuing election the reformers swept back into office and the Bill won a majority of 137 in the House of Commons. But the House of Lords lay craftily in wait and in October, 1831, they rejected it by a majority of 41. All but one of the bishops voted against it. Twenty-five years previously they had thought it their Christian duty to oppose the abolition of the slave trade: now, exhorted by the dreadful Phillpotts, Bishop of Exeter, and by the Bishop of Worcester who was only a shade less pernicious, they succeeded in blighting the hopes of the people. They numbered twenty-one. So a solid episcopal vote in favour of the Bill, surely influencing one or two lay waverers, would have saved the day and averted much bitterness.

As it was, the immediate results included the mobbing of Wellington, the knocking unconscious of Lord Londonderry, the destruction of the Duke of Newcastle's castle at Nottingham and of the Mansion House at Bristol, and the entirely understandable burning of all the bishops in effigy apart from the Bishop of Norwich who alone on the episcopal bench had bravely voted for the Bill.

Meanwhile Durham was prostrated by the death of his attractive and intelligent son, Charles. Racked by the pains in his head, which always afflicted him in times of stress, he became temporarily unbalanced. He wrote abusive letters to his father-in-law, Grey, complaining that he had been given neither an earldom nor the Foreign Office. "What a rare thing," wrote Richard Monckton Milnes, "is a grown-up mind," and there were certainly times when Durham was childish. Nor did that apply solely when, as on this occasion, he was suffering acute physical and emotional distress.

There was a specially painful example of his temporary derangement when the Government were considering how best to amend the Bill so as to resolve the problem caused

44

by the King's refusal to create enough new peers to swamp the recalcitrant House of Lords. Durham had been away in Brussels giving advice to his friend Leopold of Saxe-Coburg-Gotha on how to deal with threats from the Dutch to the newly created State of Belgium, of which Leopold had been chosen King. While he was in Brussels the Cabinet, faced by a dilemma, approved amendments to the Bill of which Durham disapproved. On December 5th, 1831, the eve of the opening of Parliament, Lord Althorp who had all along been friendly and helpful to Durham gave a dinner for his Cabinet colleagues. Durham behaved disgracefully, attacking Lord Grey, whom in reality he loved and esteemed, abusively accusing him of betrayal and incoherently blaming him for the death of his son. All present were deeply shocked and they never forgot the ill-tempered outburst. It seems that the only member of the Cabinet who forgot and forgave was the injured party, Grey himself.

After several wily defensive actions by the Lords, and a number of tergiversations by the King, who would one day agree to create enough new peers to pass the Bill and decide against it the next, the Bill did finally receive the royal assent in June, 1832. Grey had explained to the King that the choice lay between creating peers and mob violence, perhaps even revolution. So the King finally gave his consent to new creations if they should be necessary and he did so in writing. His private secretary then succeeded in persuading sufficient Tory peers to abstain as the alternative to being swamped by newly ennobled Whigs. Eighty years later, in 1911, history repeated itself in the bitter controversy over the Parliament Bill.

While the Lords were prevaricating, there had been disturbance and disgust throughout the country, but at least Durham had an opportunity to say in the Lords what he felt about Bishop Phillpotts, whose speech opposing reform consisted, he said, of "coarse and virulent invective, malignant and false insinuations and the grossest perversions of historical facts, decked out in all the choicest flowers of his well-known pamphleteering slang . . ."

The hope of the Bill's opponents had lain in the possibility

45

of Wellington being able to form an Administration. The leaders of revolutionary incitement included Francis Place, a tailor with a shop at Charing Cross. As a preliminary to insurrection he and his friends advised the people to organise a run on the banks – "To stop the Duke, go for gold" – and they advocated refusal to pay taxes. The campaign met with some success and the Bank of England was worried. Place detested the upper classes. However, he approved of Radical Jack and gave him all the assistance he could. As Professor Chester New has written: "The fact of the aristocrat-hating radical tailor of Charing Cross burning the midnight oil over material for Lord Durham's speeches in the House of Lords is not the least interesting feature of the fight for the Reform Bill."

*The Times* in one of its liberal phases supported the Bill strongly and tore its opponents to shreds. The Editor, Thomas Barnes, was under the illusion that, had it failed to pass, and had Wellington formed an Administration, the army would have been mobilised against the Radicals; he believed that the spirit of Peterloo still breathed in Tory circles. In a leading article published immediately after the Bill became an Act, Barnes declared: "Yes, the army was to be let loose upon us! Many a green or grizzled jackanapes about the clubs and public offices, and in Bond Street, was heard to declaim on the necessity of placing the Hero of Waterloo at the head of affairs when 'the edge of the sword' would settle the question in a fortnight." The Editor was evidently prone to illusions. The "Hero of Waterloo" would have been too circumspect to resort to martial law and he would certainly not have been encouraged to do so at St. James's Palace, where the strength of the still quiescent political unions was recognised. Nobody liked to be reminded of Peterloo.

Conscious that even now only one man in six (and of course no women) would be able to vote, Durham did not look upon the new Act as anything but transitional, whereas Lord John Russell, now called "Finality John", thought there was no need for further measures. Throughout the country Durham rather than Russell was hailed as a hero. However, the ink was hardly dry on the King's assent before Durham, just further bereaved by the death of his daughter Harriet, was asked to go on a mission to Russia to seek the Tsar's help in unravelling the Belgian imbroglio which, it was feared, might lead to a European war. For the sake of his friendship with King Leopold he agreed to go. He arrived at Cronstadt, where the Tsar Nicholas was inspecting his fleet, in the middle of July, 1832. Despite his radical reputation Durham, who was always punctilious in matters of protocol and could exude enormous charm when he so wished, quickly won the reactionary Tsar's liking and esteem.

His mission was successful. The Tsar paid immediate attention to his pleas, so that with both Russian and French support, and much skilful diplomacy by Grey and Palmerston, the Belgian crisis was resolved. King Leopold had every reason to be grateful to Durham. So had Leopold's niece, Princess Victoria of Kent, whose mother Durham helped by sound advice in her difficult relationship with another, less affectionate uncle of the Princess, King William IV. However, a few years later she was, as the young Queen Victoria, to fall under the spell of a man who hated Durham and helped to thwart him at the most critical time in his career, Lord Melbourne.

Returning to London from St. Petersburg, Durham became involved in disputes over the revenues of the Anglican Church of Ireland and a harsh Coercion Bill for that unhappy island. There was a row involving Stanley, the future Lord Derby, known for his outstanding eloquence as "the Rupert of Debate". Durham in his least attractive mood quarrelled with most of his colleagues, including the long-suffering Grey, especially when Grey agreed to a statement by Stanley, made for tactical reasons, that the Reform Act must be regarded as the final measure of parliamentary reform. Another daughter, Georgiana, died of consumption, at the age of nineteen, and her sorrowing father was stricken with one of his periodic blind headaches. This time it lasted for several weeks. In March, 1833 he was so ill that although he had made up his differences with Grey, he resigned his office. In recognition of his short but outstanding service to the Crown, a Sovereign who respected but disliked him conferred on him the long-desired earldom.

When, after some therapeutic months sailing at Cowes in his yacht *Louisa*, Jack, now Earl of Durham, was restored to health, the more liberal Whigs and the Radicals saw a chance of running him for Prime Minister. The possibility, which he never entertained himself, was quite widely canvassed. In fact, nothing would ever have induced him to supplant Grey, however often he might abuse that long-suffering statesman to his face. This did not deter an influential newspaper, *The Morning Chronicle*, from demanding, when Lord Grey resigned in July, 1834, that Lord Durham should be his successor; and such a choice (which only the most extreme pressure would have induced William IV to make) would have met with vociferous applause in the large, newly enfranchised cities. He would not have had the patience, the parliamentary support or the quality of leadership required by the office of Prime Minister, and in the event it was Lord Melbourne who succeeded Grey.

Lord Durham proceeded, with no good reason whatever, to quarrel publicly with the Lord Chancellor, Lord Brougham, who had formerly been his close ally in the campaign for parliamentary reform and was not only the best orator in the country but also a man of dazzling versatility. It may be that Lord Durham, quite wrongly, suspected Brougham of having engineered Grey's resignation. The ostensible cause of their quarrel was Brougham's declaration that before an attempt was made to procure further parliamentary reform careful deliberation should take precedence of action.

There can be no doubt that Brougham was right, for though he did not agree with Lord John Russell, Grey and Melbourne that the 1832 Act must be the final act in the drama, it was another thirty-five years before public opinion allowed Disraeli to introduce a wider extension of the franchise. However, this cautious attitude did not at all suit Lord Durham's impetuous temperament. He was fêted throughout the country as the prophet of progress and the euphoric climax was reached when he went to Glasgow to receive the

Freedom of the City, proceeding through cheering crowds which lined the streets for two miles. A hundred and twenty thousand people gathered to hear him speak in the open air and in the evening there was an elaborate banquet with thirty-nine toasts. It might be an age of austerity for the poor, but as the Eglinton Tournament a few years later showed, it was also an age of lavish display and extravagance.

He took this opportunity at Glasgow to declare for household suffrage – votes for all householders whatever rates they paid – for triennial parliaments and for secret ballots. The Radicals and the big political unions were delighted and the "Durham for Prime Minister" cry grew louder. On his way home to Lambton he addressed enthusiastic audiences at Lanark, Biggar, Peebles and Melrose, and a few days later he made an inflammatory speech after a dinner in his honour at Newcastle. Lord Grey was horrified and so was Lord John Russell. Durham's brother-in-law, Lord Howick, a future Colonial Secretary, considered the speeches to be those of a demagogue bidding for popular support at any price.

Nevertheless, Radical Jack was not quite as radical as his enemies and even some of his relations supposed. He had no sympathy with revolutionary ideas and would have died in the defence of the constitution. He felt that for the time being he had gone far enough in the popular cause and in 1835 he accepted an invitation to return to St. Petersburg as Ambassador. On giving him the requisite audience, the King was, Lord Durham told Lord Grey, *very* rude to him.

The last of his three daughters by Henrietta Cholmonde-ley, Frances, was married to a son of Lord Duncannon, his colleague on the Reform Bill committee, and a first cousin of Louisa. It is but one example of the closeness of patrician matrimonial circles in those days. Shortly after her father's arrival in Russia poor Frances, far away in Ireland, succumbed to the family curse of consumption. This was Lord Durham's fourth loss of a much-loved child in three years. In consequence he was as usual prostrate with physical suffering; but he pulled himself together, sent home invaluable

49

reports on Russia's military strength, persuaded Palmerston to modify his too outspoken anti-Russian statements and even prevailed on the Tsar to promise an alleviation for the cruelly oppressed Poles. He was given privileged personal access to the Tsar, he won the confidence of the Foreign Minister, he relieved a number of the grievances of British merchants and he convinced His Majesty's Government that there was no Russian threat to Turkey. He did, however, express the far-sighted view that there would one day be a threat to Persia, to Afghanistan and to India.

When he relinquished his embassy in 1837, he was deemed by the King, the Foreign Office and the Government to have been highly successful. His love of outward distinction was satisfied by King William's decision to confer on him a high order of knighthood and the Tsar stepped in with the Cross of St. Andrew. Lord Durham had sent Princess Victoria a fine edition of Milton for her birthday and her very first sovereign act, after succeeding to the throne that summer, was to invest him as a Knight Grand Cross of the Bath.

Whatever the hopes of the Radicals and reformist Liberals (as the Whigs now began to be called), Lord Durham had no further political ambitions at home. Instead there came to him an opportunity which mobilised the energy with which he always met a challenge, provided proof of his clear-sightedness and gave him a lasting claim to fame. The Prime Minister, Melbourne, did not want such a gadfly and potential firebrand to stay in the United Kingdom if he could help it. Moreover, he could not stand bad manners and he thought Lord Durham's atrocious, as to his equals they all too often were. So he invited him to go with plenary powers to Canada where the political situation was deteriorating and rebellions were taking place. Something must be urgently done to pacify the Canadian colonists, though neither Melbourne nor the majority of his colleagues were much interested in colonists or in Canada. Melbourne did, however, promise Lord Durham "the fullest and most unflinching support", words which soon rang hollow.

# 3

# Canadian Triumph

Well liked by the Tsar, by the King of the Belgians (to whom Lord Durham had given generous personal subsidies before his accession to the throne) and of course by the Radicals, Lord Durham was detested by Melbourne, the Prime Minister, no longer approved by his former collaborators, Russell and Graham, and frowned upon even by Lord Grey and Louisa's brother, Lord Howick. The majority of the nobility and gentry regarded him as a vulgar, flamboyant and irascible traitor to his class. His own blood was of the bluest, his wife's family connections illustrious, but for his detractors even those hereditary advantages, which they would normally have respected, were submerged in their resentment of political doctrines they deemed revolutionary.

In reality neither his pride of family and property nor his

occasionally distasteful eagerness for honours were based on vanity, however haughty he might sometimes be, however he might revel in glamour, ceremony and display. Pride and self-assurance are composites of arrogance, a defect which in Lord Durham's case was visible on the surface and was punished by the dislike of many of his contemporaries. It was balanced by his physical suffering and outweighed by his achievements. In fact, he was generally modest about his abilities. His outbursts of black temper, usually due to physical and emotional distress, were brief, and he did not bear grudges. His friend and close collaborator, Charles Buller, wrote that Lord Durham lacked self-confidence; and that is not incompatible with an outward display of self-assurance.

His radicalism was political, based on dedication to parliamentary reform and awareness of a changing world: it was not in any way social, though he had a genuine compassion for the poor and under-privileged, especially for those dependent on him personally like the Durham miners. Social reform – factory acts, the poor law, education – preoccupied him but little, though except in respect of trade unions his sympathies were with those supporting liberal measures and he was a strong advocate of the reform of local government.

Sensitive, never evasive and possessed of unquenchable energy when not prostrated by illness, his virtues are perhaps clearer to later generations than to his own. His affection for his family was constant and, though on several occasions he was disgracefully offensive to his father-in-law, Lord Grey, their mutual esteem did not waver. His inclination was to spoil his children, though he demanded obedience and insisted on punctuality. One person in whose eyes he could do no wrong, and to whom he was consistently faithful, was his wife, Louisa. She suffered with and for him, and when he died she had no wish to survive.

This was the man who early in 1838 agreed, at first reluctantly, to go to Canada as "Captain-General and Governor-in-Chief, for the adjustment of several questions depending in the said provinces". The "questions depending" arose from the outbreak of rebellions in Upper and Lower Canada – respectively the British and French provinces – both thoroughly badly governed. The maritime provinces of Nova Scotia, which was mainly French, New Brunswick, which was solidly British, and Prince Edward Island were peaceful; and the vast areas west of Upper Canada were still the preserve of mainly friendly Red Indians, better treated than in the United States, with isolated trading posts established by the Hudson's Bay Company. The problem was the French colonists.

That nation of shopkeepers, the British, had infiltrated for purely commercial reasons into Lower Canada (which is now the province of Quebec) and under the auspices of complacent Governors had monopolised the non-elective Executive Council with whose advice the Governor ruled. The elected Assembly of French Canadians had little power or influence. Allowed to retain their own pre-revolutionary laws and customs, and never molested in their Roman Catholic faith, the French had at first cheerfully transferred their allegiance to the British Crown when Canada was ceded to Britain by a defeated France in 1763. The French Canadians had been unmoved by the French Revolution and unaffected by its slogans. All they asked was to be left unhindered in their peaceful if primitive rural pursuits.

Then the British traders came to Quebec and Montreal and upset every kind of apple-cart. Seeing no hope of being allowed an effective say in their own affairs and alert to plans to anglicise the province, the French, or at any rate the more politically conscious among them, rebelled in 1837. They hoped for support from their republican neighbour south of the border. The French minority in Upper Canada, supported by a small but energetic British and Irish Reform group, followed suit. There were unpleasant incidents involving incursions from over the southern frontier by Americans of a ruffianly kind to whom it had long seemed logical to annex Canada to the United States. The rebellions were quashed by British troops and Canadian volunteers under the command of an able Peninsular War

53

veteran, Sir John Colborne, who had led the decisive flank attack on the Imperial Guard at the battle of Waterloo. By the time of Lord Durham's appointment, the gaols were filled by five hundred captured rebels, many liable to sentence of death for treason.

Before setting out on his mission Lord Durham recruited a staff with ideals sympathetic to his own. As his secretary he chose Charles Buller, a Liberal Member of Parliament whose frothing wit and sense of humour had tended to disguise his real abilities. As a conversationalist Buller's friendly rival was another Liberal M.P., Richard Monckton Milnes, and sometimes when they knew they would be dining at the same house they would meet at Brooks's to plan in advance brilliant "impromptus" with which to cap each other's jests. Nevertheless, beneath the surface sparkle, Buller was a man of serious intent and great intelligence.

It was as well to have in the party a man who could amuse, for Lord Durham does not seem to have had an infectious sense of humour. Indeed, that was not apparently an attribute of most nineteenth-century politicians, at any rate after the days of George Canning, though Palmerston was evidently entertaining and both Melbourne and Disraeli were witty. Perhaps the fault lies with the historians who may have been more lacking in humour than the subjects of their biographies.

Two appointments gave rise to vicious criticism at home. One was Thomas Turton, a contemporary of Lord Durham at Eton who had been divorced for seducing his sister-in-law, causing a much-publicised scandal. He was an outstanding lawyer and as Lord Durham had been promised a free hand in choosing his staff, he saw no reason to consult the Prime Minister or the Colonial Office. It was a reckless omission, by no means untrue to form.

To join him Turton had travelled home from India through the Egyptian desert with his wife, seven children, a hundred camels and twelve donkeys.

The other much-criticised choice was Edward Wakefield, who was more knowledgeable about colonial affairs than any other man in England. Unfortunately he had spent three years in prison for abducting and marrying a school-girl who was both a substantial heiress and a ward-in-chancery. He had long since reformed, but his name, like that of Turton, stank in respectable nostrils. Both these men were staunch Radicals; both were regarded with dislike and suspicion by the ruling class; and they were almost immediately the victims of a political witch-hunt such as was to become all too familiar in the second half of the following century. Neither of them, nor Lord Durham himself, accepted any remuneration from British sources, but that was only a minor obstacle in the path of the witch-hunters.

In April, 1838 Lord Durham left for Canada in a large sailing ship of the Royal Navy. He embarked not only his wife and four children and a large staff, but many crates of champagne, chests of silver, carriages and horses, a French chef and two regimental orchestras to entertain the party on board. Much thought had been given to the policy to pursue in Canada and Lord Durham had discussed at length with his staff the options available. When H.M.S. *Hastings* dropped anchor off Quebec at the end of May, 1838, more than a month after sailing from Portsmouth, having crossed the Atlantic in the face of heavy storms alternating with contrary winds, his plans were ready. He believed the solution to lie in a federation of all the Canadian provinces, but he was, as in his aspirations for parliamentary reform at home, too far-sighted and too ambitious in expecting to conquer the prejudices prevailing and to build Rome in a day.

The news of his mission had aroused excitement and hope among the French as well as the British colonists. A ceremonial entry into Quebec provided him with an opportunity for the display and grandeur he liked so much. An imposing procession was formed. With the bands playing, the cannons roaring in salute and coloured draperies hanging from every window, Lord Durham led the procession to the Castle of St. Louis, riding a white horse and dressed in a splendid uniform adorned with silver lace (instead of the usual gold). Across his chest was the collar of the Order of the Bath and the assembled crowds were dazzled by the magnificence of the procession and of its handsome central figure.

He lost no time. He dismissed all but one of the members of the Lieutenant-Governor's Executive Council in Lower Canada; but he did so with such charm and tact that none of them took umbrage. He declared an amnesty for those rebels still in the gaols with the sole exception of eight of the more notorious ring-leaders. The enthusiasm in Quebec and Montreal was immediate and vociferous, even among the British businessmen who had previously dominated the Government. Those in control of Upper Canada, which is now Ontario, were less sure, for they were a "Family Compact" which had been enjoying a monopoly of power comparable with the rotten borough system in Britain.

Lord Durham then made an error which was to cost him dear. He had no intention of executing the eight rebel leaders excluded from the amnesty and it would seem harsh to their friends and relations if they were transported to Botany Bay, quite apart from the problem of arranging shipment. They had resorted to violence, but their crimes arose from idealism. So he hit on what seemed the bright idea of issuing an ordinance by which the eight were exiled to Bermuda. He wrote to the Governor of the island recommending that they be allowed reasonable freedom but included in his ordinance a proviso that if they returned to Canada they would be executed. Unfortunately for Lord Durham, Bermuda was not within his jurisdiction and it later transpired that his action, however sensible, was technically illegal.

Having disposed of this problem, as he thought satisfactorily, he turned his attention to the United States, whence marauding forays and acts of piracy by Americans, and by Canadian rebels who had taken refuge south of the border, were frequent and provocative. He sent his brother-in-law, Charles Grey[1], to Washington with a tactful message to

[1] Younger son of Lord Grey; later Private Secretary to the Prince Consort and to Queen Victoria.

President Van Buren which was well received. On visiting Niagara he gave a lavish dinner party for 260 people, amongst whom he included forty guests from the American bank of the St. Lawrence. He took the unprecedented step of formally proposing the health of the President of the United States, adding that he hoped there would never be any cause for collision between Britain and the United States, "and as they are brothers in blood, I trust they will always remain brothers in sentiment and feeling". One of the American newspapers reported that "The Earl was as familiar as though he had been one of our citizens."

The Durhams then crossed the river on to American soil at Buffalo, despite warnings of danger by Sir John Colborne and the Canadian authorities. He and his staff wore full uniform and the fears for their safety proved groundless. They were received in Buffalo with both respect and friendliness.

Charles Buller wrote of the great reception at Niagara:

I have often said to those who used to dilate on the seven or eight hundred pounds that were spent in the course of Lord Durham's visit to Niagara that, considering the results attributable to it, a million of money would have been a cheap price for the single glass of wine which Lord Durham drank to the health of the American President.

A less appreciative commentator was Ensign Charles Colville[1], a young officer of the 85th Foot stationed at Toronto. He wrote to his father, one of Wellington's Generals in the Peninsula and at Waterloo:

Lord Durham when at Niagara lived at the rate of £100 per diem. He gave a ball to all those who chose to go, Yankees included, at which 360 bottles of champagne were consumed.

[1] Charles John, subsequently 1st Viscount, 11th Baron Colville of Culross, K.T.

Colville, who was a future Conservative Chief Whip in the House of Lords, had a distaste for Radicals.

Buller was right. One result of such expensive diplomacy was a highly favourable press coverage in the United States where "The Lord" as they called him was hailed as a hero; another, much more important, result was an order sent from the White House to the American General on the frontier to prevent incursions into Canada and arrest those who attempted them. The President invited Lord Durham to pay a state visit to Washington. Later developments precluded the visit, to which he was looking forward, but American relations with both Canada and Great Britain were greatly improved.

On the way back to Quebec there was a short interlude for relaxation. Lord Durham's suite included Edward Ellice and his wife Jane, who kept a diary. Ellice, Member of Parliament for St. Andrews, son of Lord Durham's long-standing associate "Bear" Ellice, and a first cousin of Louisa, had come to Canada partly as a political secretary (though a less assiduous one than Charles Buller) and partly to visit the huge estates, totalling more than 400,000 acres, which the Ellice family owned in Canada and the United States. Among these possessions was the seigneurie of Beauharnois, with a house, long neglected, infested with bedbugs, but beautifully situated on the shore of Lac St. Louis where the St. Lawrence and Ottawa rivers meet. Absentee British landlords were not just peculiar to Ireland.

Lord and Lady Durham arrived to stay at Beauharnois, self-invited, shortly after the triumphant banquet at Niagara and the visit to Buffalo. They brought with them their four children and their large suite, as well as a military escort which could only be accommodated in the barns. The Ellices themselves had to take rooms in the neighbouring house of a well-known rebel, whose brother was one of the eight unpardonable ones exiled in Bermuda. After his arrival Lord Durham received a deputation on the green in front of the house and had to reply in French which, he told Jane Ellice, he thought rather hard on him. "Fortunately," she wrote, "he is in great good humour."

The following day he was not. Some of the party returned from an excursion late for dinner, "which raised His Excellency's ire. To revenge himself he left us waiting for twenty minutes and did not open his mouth to a soul during dinner." Afterwards he cancelled a proposed expedition on the lake in an Indian canoe and would not let Louisa take part either, though the children and some of the suite were eventually allowed to set forth in a fleet of canoes manned by Iroquois Indians who paddled at a great pace, singing as they went.

On the following morning Lord Durham had one of his severe headaches, which Jane Ellice thought an excuse for his ill-temper the previous evening; but he had recovered sufficiently to accompany her in an Indian canoe later in the day and to be amused when one of the Iroquois referred to Queen Victoria as "the Great English Squaw". Jane ended her account of the visit with: "There is one great charm about Lord D. – If he has been unreasonable or angry with anyone he always makes an apology somehow or another, which must be difficult for a proud, reserved man."

By the end of July, 1838, all seemed to be set fair. Lord Durham had only been able to spend ten days in Upper Canada, including a visit to Toronto where, wrote Louisa, "We were rather struck by the appearance of the streets which seemed to be better built and to consist of better houses than in any place we had seen." Charles Colville, who was in the Guard of Honour, was invited to dine with Durham at Government House, Toronto, and reported to his father: "He was very well received here, notwithstanding the general amnesty not having increased his popularity."

The French in the lower province, initially so welcoming, began to complain that he listened too much to the British in Montreal and Quebec. They resented his choice as an adviser of Adam Thom, an influential member of the Commission on Municipal Government, who wanted to anglicise the institutions of Lower Canada. However, they gladly attended the levées and banquets he gave in Quebec. Louisa told her mother that the ladies "were smarter than I expected, but seemed in a great fright". On one occasion the principal lady present, whom Lord Durham took into dinner, "ate *jelly* with her knife".

There was trouble with Sir George Arthur, Lieutenant-Governor of Upper Canada, who listened too much to the ruling clique in that province and sought to deny the Governor General's right to pardon political prisoners in Arthur's custody. "Meaureau was hanged at Fort Niagara last Monday," wrote Charles Colville on August 3rd – a clear indication that the amnesty was being disregarded.

The quality of mercy had been quite severely strained in Upper Canada, for Sir George Arthur's convictions were not at all the same as Lord Durham's. Moreover, life for the British troops sent there to keep order and suppress rebellion was harsh, and desertions were frequent. In the course of one year the 15th Foot suffered over 140, and in the 24th Foot 110 men deserted during 1836–37. A few rejoined the Colours, a few were caught and flogged or sentenced to long years of hard labour or transportation to Botany Bay; but the majority of deserters accepted inducements to take refuge in the United States where they were inveigled into working in the insalubrious lead mines, a fate they found even harsher than serving in the British army. In contrast to the line regiments the better disciplined Grenadiers only recorded seven desertions in the four and a half years they served in Canada. As for the rebels, when they were caught in Upper Canada they were frequently executed, even if they were American citizens, for though it was difficult to persuade French Canadian juries to convict, in the British province the problem scarcely arose. "The Court Martial sitting at Montreal is not half so summary or decisive as the two sitting in the Upper Province," wrote Charles Colville deprecatingly.

A commission was established to examine Crown lands and feudal tenures (a survival from pre-revolutionary France), another to make recommendations on education, a third to consider municipal institutions and yet another to study the judicial system. Lord Durham also set in train the construction of a canal to improve access from the Great Lakes to the St. Lawrence river. Then in August, out of an apparently clear blue sky, a cyclone approached.

The problems with Sir George Arthur and the French in Lower Canada were local irritations. The cyclone crossed the Atlantic from Westminster. Despite hostile parliamentary comments and their own strongly expressed disapproval of the two counsellors with an unsavoury past, Turton and Wakefield, both Melbourne and the Colonial Secretary, Lord Glenelg, had sent Lord Durham warm congratulations on his early achievements and on the high regard in which the Canadians evidently held him. But that astute and seldom scrupulous lawyer, Lord Brougham, who still bore a grudge dating from the undignified and quite unnecessary squabble over the speed of further parliamentary reform (for which Lord Durham was largely to blame), discovered that the clauses in Lord Durham's ordinance deporting the eight rebels to the pleasant, if fever-ridden, island of Bermuda and threatening them with execution if they returned were illegal.

There were debates in both Houses of Parliament. After an initial defence by Melbourne, who disliked Brougham as much as he did Lord Durham, Parliament voted to disallow the ordinance to which Melbourne and Glenelg had given "their most entire approval". The Government, fearful of defeat, recoiled from the obvious solution of introducing a short Bill to legalise the Bermudan episode, leaving intact the main part of the ordinance which the Law Officers had declared unexceptionable. Instead they weakly capitulated to Brougham who had added to his Bill an act of indemnity for those who had obeyed Lord Durham's commands. It was a deliberate humiliation for Lord Durham. Brougham's spiteful initiative succeeded, though it did nothing to enhance his reputation.

The Canadians, in Upper and Lower Canada and in the Maritimes, were infuriated. Some even spoke of seceding, like the American colonists in 1776. The British Parliament in its arrogance and folly had failed to digest that earlier

61

lesson. Indeed, only a minority at Westminster were at all interested in a colonial empire. Britannia was primarily concerned with ruling the waves round the British Isles and on the route to India. In the words of Edmund Burke spoken sixty years before: "A great empire and little minds go ill together."

A torrent of addresses and petitions flowed to the Castle in Quebec and there were huge demonstrations in support of Lord Durham who must have found it agreeable to see Brougham and Melbourne burned in effigy. Disowned and humiliated by the British Parliament, he decided to resign; but there was unfinished work to do and for once he did not act impetuously, nor did he intend to wash his hands of Canadian interests.

On October 9th he issued a proclamation. As required by Parliament he withdrew the ordinance and announced the Act of Indemnity. That meant, he said, the continued validity of the amnesty, but without any exceptions, "for I cannot recall the irrevocable pledge of Her Majesty's mercy". The principal troublemakers, exiled to Bermuda but now free to resume their activities, could return to Canada. Lord Durham made a powerful defence of his actions since his arrival in the previous May and wrote, referring to the British Government and Parliament:

> From the very commencement of my task the minutest details have been exposed to incessant criticism, in a spirit which has evinced an entire ignorance of the state of this country.

The Ministers of the Crown had made it clear to him "that my authority is inadequate for the emergency which called it into existence".

This proclamation was received with fervent applause throughout Canada and with equally fervent indignation in British governing circles. *The Times*, no longer in radical mood, called Lord Durham "The Lord High Seditioner" and one of the few who came down in his favour was John

Stuart Mill, the much-respected protagonist of liberty. The Colonial Secretary, Lord Glenelg, in a despatch expressing stern governmental disapproval, wrote "I have received Her Majesty's commands to signify to Your Lordship Her Majesty's disapprobation of your proclamation of the 9th October." The nineteen-year-old Queen, spellbound by Melbourne, had conveniently forgotten Lord Durham's kindness to her and her mother in days gone by. She had only been on the throne a year, was still unmarried and was politically inexperienced. Melbourne rated expediency above loyalty to a colleague, and the Queen, soothed by his avuncular manner, was more disposed to accept ministerial advice without demur than ever she was in later years.

All the same this royal reproof gave Durham much distress, for there was no loyaller subject and he did not expect from Queen Victoria personally what might well have come from William IV. On returning home, Louisa's first act was to resign her post as a Lady in Waiting, a gesture by which the Queen was not amused.

A week before the Durhams departed, the officer commanding the Brigade of Guards made a speech at a dinner given in Lord Durham's honour at Quebec, praising him personally and supporting his policy. He went so far as to say that the welfare of Canada was being sacrificed on the altar of British party politics, a view which was supported by most of his brother officers even though it implied indirect criticism of Queen Victoria herself.

The Ellices who travelled from Beauharnois to say goodbye dined each night at the Castle. One evening Jane noted: "His Excellency was attired in plain clothes for a treat, and how much more becoming to him than that ugly red and silver uniform he always wears here." Her own clothes were a source of worry: "Large party at dinner. I intended to be very smart in my new blue velvet gown, but it didn't fit to E. E.'s [her husband's] liking so I was obliged to take it off in double quick time. However, we were in time for dinner, so I did not care." Finally: "Saw a large wolf which has been made a present to Lord D. and is going to

Lambton to take up its quarters with the bears." Edward and Jane Ellice returned to Beauharnois just in time to be caught at the centre of a renewed outbreak of rebellion, to have their house devastated and their village burned, to be imprisoned in utter misery for several days and only narrowly to escape with their lives.

On November 1st the Durhams sailed for home, leaving Quebec through dense, silent and mournful crowds of well-wishers. Some of the staff, including Charles Buller, remained temporarily behind to further the work of the commissions set up to make recommendations on municipal reform, general education, the laws relating to real estate and commerce, and the administration of justice. Seeds of vital importance for the future had been well sown; but Lord Durham was leaving Canada after only five months, surely the shortest proconsulate in the history of the British Empire, but no less surely one of the most fruitful in its results.

A few days after he sailed the new rebellion by which the Ellices were trapped broke out in Lower Canada and there were two serious incursions from the United States, which the American authorities were unable to prevent. Charles Colville told his father that "upwards of 100 rebels were killed at Prescott. There was not a single Canadian among them: they were composed of Yankees with a good many Poles and Spaniards. The army here, both officers and men, have the most violent hatred for the Yankees and long to have a slap at them." That was the sentiment held in Upper Canada, but it was not one which Durham and his entourage shared. Sir John Colborne, whom Lord Durham had invited to assume full civil and military powers, successfully suppressed the risings which lasted but a few days. This time less mercy was shown to the insurgents, who had committed a number of atrocities, though out of ninety-nine found guilty of high treason only twelve were executed. Early in January, 1839, Charles Colville, reporting on the trials of the rebels, told his father: "I saw one of them hanged at London [Ontario] the other day; he was a fine fellow, acknowledged the justice of his sentence; gave some good advice to his fellow-prisoners; and died like a man."

A few days earlier Charles had been detailed to see three soldiers in his regiment flogged, but he was evidently unmoved by it all and happily went off shooting with several brother officers in a neighbouring forest, where one of his companions peppered him with shot. In the following August he noted that his regiment had lost twenty-five by desertion in that month alone. "I don't think it will be put a stop to till the punishment of death is enforced," he commented.

The passage home was nightmarish for the Durhams. The ship, aptly named *Inconstant*, ran ashore once, caught fire twice and was buffeted for three weeks by fierce and unrelenting gales. In addition, Lord Durham was prostrated by migraine and neuralgia, the usual result of emotional strain. The ship reached the shelter of Plymouth harbour at the end of November. For four days the sea was too rough and Lord Durham was too ill to disembark, but when he did so he was received with rapture by the crowds. There were many who hoped he would oust Melbourne from the leadership of his party and himself become Prime Minister with overwhelming popular support. "Durham and Reform" had been a slogan widely disseminated in Britain four years previously and more recently in Canada; but he had no intention of campaigning against the Government, however shamefully they had let him down. He had set his hand to a Canadian plough which he did not intend to relinquish. He went to No. 13 Cleveland Row and with the help of his staff, including Charles Buller who soon returned from Canada, worked tirelessly on the preparation of what is known to history as the Durham Report. He saw nobody but the members of his late staff and he devoted himself feverishly to drafting.

He had regretfully abandoned the idea of an immediate Federation, since he realised that the Maritime Provinces were resolutely opposed to it. There was obviously no chance that his still more ambitious hope of one legally unified Canadian Dominion would be accepted for years to come. So he felt obliged to fall back on the lesser but more practical alternative of uniting Upper and Lower Canada.

He was determined that the new constitution should in no way resemble that of the United States with its separation of powers, its election of judges and sheriffs and other late eighteenth-century refinements of political theory. Canada was to be endowed with an independent judiciary and with parliamentary government. The Governor's executive council was to be converted into a Cabinet, the members of which would sit in the Assembly and be responsible for their actions to its democratically elected majority. In other words he proposed a system of government for Canada approximating to that of the mother country.

This blueprint for responsible government did eventually prevail in Canada, and it became the basis on which all the self-governing countries of the British Empire, including India, shed colonial rule. Those, mainly in Africa, which chose to discard this pattern soon succumbed to dictatorship.

By an exhaustive effort the Durham Report was completed at the end of January, 1839. It contained useful insertions and appendices written by Buller, Turton and Wakefield in their specialised fields. However, the drive, inspiration and much of the drafting was by Lord Durham himself, though the *Dictionary of National Biography* erroneously gives most of the credit to Buller. The Report was accepted by Melbourne, searching for a means of diverting attention from the Government's other problems, and he proposed that a Bill be immediately presented to unite the two Canadas. This was temporarily thwarted, but Sir Robert Peel, leading the Opposition in the House of Commons, came down in favour of it and finally there was no serious objection in either House. Peel was one of the few politicians who was sensitive to colonial feelings. On one occasion he had said: "You have got another Ireland growing up in every colony you possess."

Lord Durham's bolder aspirations were fulfilled in slow

stages, partly because the Canadians feared that too great an independence from the United Kingdom might be an inducement to annexation by the United States. Thus a close association with Britain, then militarily and economically stronger than the young American republic, was an invaluable safeguard, especially as the gradual replacement of sail by steam meant that the transport of troops from Britain to Canada would be greatly accelerated. By the time Lord Durham went home the *Great Western* was already crossing the Atlantic in the miraculously short time of thirteen days. Delay was also due to the Tories in Upper Canada kicking hard against the project of responsible government based on the subordination of the executive to the legislature.

It was decreed in London that all matters relating to constitutional changes, foreign relations, trade and the disposal of public lands should be reserved for decision by the British Parliament. Nevertheless, bit by bit the Report was implemented and it would have been pleasing to Durham to know that a strong element of responsible government was introduced in 1846 when his daughter Mary's husband, Lord Elgin, was Governor General and his brother-in-law, Lord Howick, Secretary of State for the Colonies. Finally, confederation was established in 1867 by Disraeli who many years before had sought Lord Durham's help in finding a seat in Parliament. Thus, a generation after Lord Durham sailed away from Quebec, Canada, "the Great Dominion", became the first British colony to be given what was effectively independence under the Crown.

Lord Durham was not to see all this. The stimulus of his strenuous labours in the preparation of the Report had revived his spirits and temporarily restored his health. He spoke several times in the House of Lords in support of the Canadian Unity Bill which, like the Reform Bill of 1832, he correctly regarded as only a first instalment. He tore in shreds noble lords who dared to renew the attack on his friend and collaborator, Turton; he gave invaluable advice to an old Radical associate, Poulett Thomson, appointed to be his successor in Canada; he made up his quarrel with Melbourne and even with Brougham; and he found time as Governor of the New Zealand Company to support Edward Wakefield who was now devoting himself self-effacingly to the colonisation of those long-neglected islands. It is ironical that Lambton Harbour in the North Island, so called in his honour, was later submerged in the city of Wellington, named to commemorate one of Lambton's strongest political opponents, who had never been remotely concerned with New Zealand.

The burst of energy did not last long. In May 1840 he was found to be suffering from consumption, the malign fiend which had carried off his father, his first wife, and four of his children. Retiring to his house at Cowes, he grew steadily weaker and on July 28th, 1840, he died, aged forty-eight, a few days after the Canadian Unity Bill received the Royal Assent and the first step was thus taken to implement the Durham Report. He had been a little too far-sighted, always aspiring to reach immediately goals that were desirable but unattainable in the prevailing circumstances. He was a generation ahead of his contemporaries. The marks he left in the sands of time were well imprinted, but except in Canada later generations have passed by without noticing them.

A year later his wife Louisa, desolated by his death, joined him in the family vault in the Collegiate Church at Chester-le-Street, where the body of their beautiful and promising elder son, Charles, had been lying for ten years. Apart from the replica of a Greek temple, subscribed for by neighbours and built on a hill near Lambton Castle, there are no statues or monuments to commemorate Radical Jack, and the only trace left of him in London is a portrait hanging on a wall of the Reform Club in Pall Mall. However, in the parliaments of the British Commonwealth, and above all in Canada, Sir Christopher Wren's epitaph at St. Paul's Cathedral applies also to Durham: *Si monumentum requiris, circumspice* – If you want a monument, look around you.

# Part Two

# 4

# New Generations

———————

When Louisa died in 1841, she left behind three daughters and one thirteen-year-old son, George, who had become the 2nd Earl of Durham the previous year. They were the sole survivors of Radical Jack's eight children.

There was little that was remarkable about George or his sisters. As the baby of the family he had been cherished, and even before his more obviously attractive elder brother died his father had always found time to play with him, as he did with all his children. When he was nine he was taken on the rough sea voyage to Quebec with his parents, his three sisters and a tutor. While he was there he had a serious illness and his father, mindful of all the previous tragedies, was deeply anxious. However, he recovered in time for the still more unpleasant return journey a few weeks after his tenth birthday.

Ten years younger than his brother Charles, who had died when George was three, he grew up in "the Hungry Forties" when the failure of the potato crop devastated the Irish peasantry. Thousands emigrated, carrying their bitterness overseas with them, a bitterness which has been handed down from generation to generation in the United States. In the towns of England and southern Scotland the children of the Industrial Revolution, increasing rapidly in number, (for sex was their parents' sole unfettered diversion), were lodged in squalor, uneducated and underfed. Almost as soon as they could walk they were forced to work inhumanly long hours for skinflint wages; and the public authorities were guilty of a horrifying exploitation of pauper apprentices. The Chartists, demanding more radical reforms than Parliament was prepared to offer, pulled down the railings round Hyde Park and organised inflammatory meetings. In Europe, where discontent was still greater than in Britain, the rumblings of revolution grew louder year by year.

From all this George was sheltered at Lambton and at Howick, his mother's family home, where, since he had no parents to guide him in his formative years, it might have been expected that his mother's family would attend to his political education. His grandfather, the former Prime Minister, Earl Grey, died in 1845; his mother's eldest brother, Lord Howick, was busily occupied in London as Secretary of State for the Colonies, and his own eldest sister Mary, wife of Lord Elgin, was away in Canada where her husband was Governor General. George declared himself, doubtless for hereditary reasons, a strong supporter of the Liberal Party, but the knowledge of current affairs which he should have acquired from the Grey family was scanty, even though most of his mother's numerous brothers and sisters were bright and intelligent.

He was not sent away to a public school or university and nobody seems to have encouraged him to have cultural interests. There was no Dr. Beddoes to stimulate his intellectual development as the good Doctor had his father's forty years before. Initially, his great estates and his coal mines were well administered for him by able and honest agents; but he knew nothing of the harsh realities of the 1840s and there was no one to stir the social conscience which had been so marked a feature of his father and both his grand-fathers. Like that remarkable character Gallio in the Acts of the Apostles, he "cared for none of these things", perhaps because he was given no opportunity to do so.

When he grew up he was duly appointed Lord Lieutenant of Durham and Lieutenant-Colonel of the Northumberland Rifle Volunteers, distinctions illustrating his status rather than his activities. As a boy he had closely resembled his father, but when he reached maturity George did not have his father's or his brother's startling good looks. He was passably handsome with wide-set eyes, a well-shaped face and body, and the drooping moustache favoured in Victorian times by those who had neither beards nor side-whiskers. Originality of thought, enterprise and intelligence skipped his generation. He did not learn what Lord Grey and Radical Jack would assuredly have taught him, that great wealth carries great responsibilities, nor was there anyone to instil the other high-minded principles in which his parents and grandparents believed. He was by no means an alert or conscientious mine owner, but he was far from mean. After his death in 1879 the Newcastle Town Council declared there would be "enduring remembrance of his private beneficence".

To begin with he was even richer than his father, for in one year alone, 1862, the Lambton lands and collieries showed a profit of £362,000, and that, in days when there was neither income tax nor surtax, was the equivalent of at least £10 million after tax in the 1980s. There should have been no question of jogging along. However, in due course he employed an agent who had neither the ability nor the unselfseeking integrity of his father's friend and supporter, Henry Morton, and as the years went by the collieries, starved of good management and new investment, became decreasingly profitable. Neither George nor his agent did anything about it and before the end of the century the collieries were actually showing losses. All the same, George still had plenty of money to finance a racing stable, bring up a large family and live in a high degree of comfort.

In 1854, at the age of twenty-five, he had married Beatrix, one of the seven daughters of the Duke and Duchess of Abercorn. She and her six good-looking sisters all married dukes, marquesses or earls, eschewing mere viscounts and barons. So their mother, "Granny Abercorn" as later generations called her, was known as the Mother of the Peerage.

George adored Beatrix. Her dowry was not money, but another strain of great good looks. Luckily the Lambtons were not superstitious; for not only did George's mother, Louisa Grey, come from a family of thirteen, but so did Beatrix Hamilton; and Beatrix herself produced thirteen children. Subsequently her son Freddy married the most attractive of thirteen Bulteels whose sisters in turn married into the thirteen-strong Grenfells. There were thus five closely related families all of thirteen children.

Perhaps Beatrix Durham would have exceeded the norm; but the effort of bearing thirteen sons and daughters in fifteen years killed her before any of them were fully grown-up. She left George distraught. He had always been shy and reserved, and when his wife died he withdrew into the furthest recesses of his shell. He took even less interest in politics, national or local, and devoted himself to racing and field sports. Short-tempered though he sometimes was, he remained a generous and affectionate father all his life and supplied each of his children with horses, dogs and every sporting facility; but their early training was more in coverts than in the classroom. Unfortunately one of his sons, Charles, shot his father's eye out and is said to have been the original "Bag Dad". It fell to his eldest daughter, another Beatrix, aged only fourteen when her mother died, to preside over the upbringing of her brothers and sisters. In due course she escaped and married Lord Pembroke, owner of Wilton and thirty thousand fertile acres in Wiltshire.

Not content with his own broad acres at Lambton, which was losing its rural aspect, George built a comfortable but ugly house, Fenton, in Northumberland, where he acquired thirty thousand acres. It was in good hunting and shooting country and far removed from industrial pollution. There he and his children spent a great deal of the year in surroundings more congenial to them than Lambton Castle. Such was the family prestige and such, despite his dedication to sport rather than public service, was his personal standing with the local population that when he died at the age of fifty-one, all business was suspended in Durham and twelve thousand people turned out to watch the mile-long funeral procession.

Some of his thirteen children were enterprising, original and intelligent, though only two, the Duchess of Leeds and Lady Robert Cecil, were even mildly artistic and intellectual. Of the two, Nelly Cecil had by far the more sprightly intellect. They were nearly all unusual and through them the Lambton characteristics, a blend of forcefulness and eccentricity, of drive and indolence, of indifference to the opinions of other people and of moral courage, were widely diffused. Also, perhaps from Radical Jack, they inherited critical faculties which could be a little too sharp.

The eldest sons were identical twins, Jack and Freddy, born when the Crimean War was at its height and Lord Aberdeen was Prime Minister. They were handsome and elegant. In addition Jack had, if he chose to display it, a fair share of his grandfather's charm and was well liked in all ranks of society. When, in 1879, aged twenty-four and a Lieutenant in the Coldstream Guards, he succeeded to the earldom and to the still substantial Lambton fortune, there was no lack of ambitious mothers and aunts who saw in him an exceptionally desirable match for their daughters or nieces. One of those with the most relentless aspirations was Lady Gerard, wife of a man well known in racing circles. She had a beautiful niece called Ethel Milner who was, she decided, to be the new Lord Durham's bride. The fact that

Ethel was deeply in love with a comparatively impecunious officer in the army was considered by Lady Gerard to be immaterial.

Jack, who had himself been recently disappointed in love, was lured by Lady Gerard's advocacy into proposing to the unhappy Ethel, but until the wedding day he was not allowed to be alone with her. He did comment that she was strangely silent, but Lady Gerard insisted that that was only because she was so much in love with him. It was not until after the wedding that the horror of the situation became clear to him: she was insane.

On their honeymoon their carriage ran over a child and this understandably unnerved her. Returning to Lambton Castle, she had her monthly period and showed such signs of hysteria at the sight of blood that her husband unwisely, but doubtless with the best intentions, plunged her into a cold bath. She leaped out of it screaming and ran naked round the Castle to the consternation of the servants. As there were no signs of recovery, but indeed further deterioration, the only thing to do was to place her in a home. There she lived, quietly mad, to a great old age. Divorce was out of the question, for it was not till 1939, eleven years after Jack's death, that insanity was accepted as grounds for it; and as the marriage had presumably been consummated during the honeymoon an annulment was ruled out. He did apply to the court for a declaration of nullity as soon as his wife's insanity was pronounced incurable, but after a trial lasting a week he was said by the judge not to have established his case, clear though it was to most people that he had. Jack Durham was condemned to a life if not of celibacy at least of matrimonial void.

He made several further efforts to have the law changed, but it was not until the 1930s when A. P. Herbert took up the cause of divorce on grounds of insanity that Parliament accepted what was obviously just and humane. Jack did have one illegitimate son, but he did not, as the Cholmondeleys had done in the case of Radical Jack's first wife, Henrietta, give the child his name. Since this son could never succeed, Durham would perhaps have been unwise to saddle him with a name which might lead to false hopes. Moreover, although Durham took trouble with the boy he turned out to be a problem child.

Like his father and all Lambtons Durham was devoted to the Turf. It was indeed an obsession. He began owning race-horses in 1881, two years after his father died. He built a large stud, was soon a Steward of the Jockey Club and ran his horses with limited success at all the major race-meetings. It was not until 1927, a year before he died, that he had his first classic winner when his filly, *Beam*, won the Oaks.

In days when the rules and regulations relating to horse-racing tended to be lax, his own views were strict. In 1887 he carried his principles to the extent of making a speech at the Gimcrack Dinner in the course of which he accused another member of the Jockey Club, Sir George Chetwynd, and his jockey of pulling a well-fancied horse. Sir George sued for slander. As the law suit for which both sides employed eminent Queen's Counsel proceeded, London society was sharply divided. Some, including the Prince of Wales and the Duke of Beaufort, stood by Sir George; others, such as a pillar of the Turf, Lord Marcus Beresford, later trainer for both Edward VII and George V, admired Durham's courage and believed, rightly, that his action would have a beneficial effect on racing standards. The case was bitterly fought. It seemed at first to be going Chetwynd's way, but in the end the evidence swung in Durham's favour. Sir George won a farthing damages for slander, but his reputation on the Turf was destroyed and he retired altogether from racing. The jockey's licence was withdrawn, but when it was eventually restored it is pleasing to know that his first mount was given to him by Durham on one of his own horses; and he subsequently rode a Derby winner.

In common with his brothers Jack Durham was reticent. An illustration of his family characteristic was given to Richard Molyneux, a well-known soldier and courtier who was wounded at the battle of Omdurman and given a skin graft from the arm of Winston Churchill. Molyneux was invited by Jack Durham to stay for Christmas, a feast for which all the thirteen brothers and sisters assembled at Lambton Castle. He was sitting in the drawing room talking to his host when the door opened to admit a new arrival whom Molyneux did not know. This man greeted nobody, looked neither to right nor left, and walked straight to a table where he sat down and began to write a letter. "Who is that?" asked Molyneux. "My brother D'Arcy," replied Durham, showing not the least surprise. It transpired that D'Arcy had not seen his family since the preceding Christmas. Many years later, when D'Arcy was old and ailing, his nephew Johnny and his great-nephew Tony travelled to Brockham in Surrey to see him. After greeting them, he said: "Hadn't you better be going: you might miss your train."

In September, 1914, Durham wrote in a flowing, scholarly hand (which belied his lack of scholarship) to his niece, Lady Ellesmere, to whom he was especially devoted, to console her on the death of one of her brothers who had been killed in action. In his letter, he said: "I hope he knew how fond I was of him. We are all reserved; and sometimes have to regret that we were not more demonstrative." That applied as much to most of his relations as to himself.

He played a larger part in politics and in local affairs than had his father, but he separated himself from Mr. Gladstone over Irish Home Rule and he vigorously opposed Lloyd George's 1910 budget which introduced what were then considered swingeing increases in taxation. He was Lord Lieutenant of Durham for forty-five years, Chancellor of the University and in one year Mayor of the City of Durham. He was active in the county, and respected throughout the north of England. He took a continuous interest in cattle-breeding and was responsible for crossing shorthorns, then the most familiar sight in English fields, with Aberdeen Angus. All the ladies from Queen Alexandra and Queen Mary downwards, partly, no doubt, because he was so good-looking, were devoted to him.

When war broke out in 1914, he engaged himself

effectively in the affairs of the local regiments and Territorials. In 1915 he warned that if the 6th and 7th Durham Regiments were amalgamated they would mutiny, and the military authorities, initially insensitive to "Geordie" feelings, were persuaded to cancel the amalgamation just in time.

He also became a courtier. Mr. Gladstone had originally appointed him a political Lord in Waiting to Queen Victoria, which involved his speaking for the Government in the Lords. But it was an appointment that lapsed when he rebelled over Home Rule. Until 1914 the Great Officers of State were political appointments, apart from the Earl Marshal and Lord Great Chamberlain whose offices were hereditary. This custom dated back to days before the Reform Bill when a high appointment at Court brought with it a sure guarantee of the recipient's rotten boroughs and local patronage. In King Edward VII's reign Liberal grandees were in short supply. Crewe, Carrington, Elgin and Ripon were in the Cabinet, and so Mr. Asquith gladly proposed Durham as Lord Steward of the Household. King George V, who approved of him (and of his racing interest), invited him to carry part of the insignia at his Coronation and, as the newly appointed Lord Steward, to accompany him to the famous 1911 Durbar in India. He was made a Knight of the Garter and a Privy Councillor, and although he was not by temperament an active politician he was, unlike his father, quite a frequent attender at the House of Lords. After the War, unable to reconcile himself to the Lloyd George Liberals, he switched his allegiance to the Conservatives, declaring that Mr. Stanley Baldwin "upheld the views of the old and properly described Liberal Party".

Jack Durham had been the victim of his own and his father's inattention to the family's financial interests. Perhaps if Radical Jack had lived longer, things might have been different, for he had always been deeply interested in his collieries. He felt a personal responsibility for the welfare of the miners and the modernisation of the mines, and he had an agent of the highest quality. The misfortune was not only that his son, George, inherited when he was twelve, and his grandson when he was twenty-four, but that at least until the First World War – and in many cases still later – a gentleman did not involve himself personally in business matters. The owner of lands or mines had one or more agents, who might or might not be competent and honourable men, while legal, financial and accountancy matters were entrusted to "men of business" who called the proprietor "My Lord" and were not the kind of people His Lordship invited to stay or mixed with socially. The younger sons of a great family went into the army, the navy, the diplomatic service, the Church, or, if sufficiently endowed, the House of Commons. There were one or two banking families, such as the Barings and the Rothschilds, who were socially acceptable, but generally speaking "The City" and commerce were taboo.

Lord Randolph Churchill's younger son was blackballed for the Turf Club in London because he was a stockbroker, and my own father felt obliged to offer his resignation to the Royal Yacht Squadron at Cowes because on abandoning the acceptable profession of barrister he accepted a job in the City. His resignation was only declined because his father had been a pillar of the Squadron and he was about to marry the daughter of an important Cabinet Minister.

When such conventions held sway, Durham and his neighbouring coal owner, Lord Londonderry, were not disposed to involve themselves personally in the management of their underground properties. Nor were they much concerned except in a very general way with the welfare of the miners. In 1885 low wages and bad conditions in the mines resulted in a bitter strike. One large coal owner, James Joicey, made use of his own newspaper, the *Newcastle Daily Leader*, to denounce the harsh terms demanded by the majority of the coal owners for a settlement. He was the grandson of a miner in one of the Lambton pits and had acquired his wealth by hard work, enterprise and business acumen. He declared at a meeting that the men were not animals and had the right to decent treatment. Durham is alleged to have replied: "I dare say *with your background,* you think you know these things." Whether he actually used those words, or whether it was an unsubstantiated report, is uncertain; but it is certainly what he thought and, supported by Londonderry, he showed his hostility to Joicey by launching an unsuccessful campaign to discredit him as the Liberal candidate for Chester-le-Street in 1885. Ten years later the Lambton–Joicey relationship was sour indeed.

What Durham owned was in size and value the equivalent of a great industrial company, but the owner regarded himself primarily as a beneficiary. Details of exploitation and maintenance must be left to middle-class professionals. In many families this philosophy was disastrous. It was a justification for the nationalisation of coal royalties by Stanley Baldwin and of the mines themselves by the Labour Party after 1945.

By the 1890s the once so remunerative Lambton collieries were in a sorry state. Investment had been withheld for many years, the agent was idle and incompetent and almost certainly dishonest, and coal prices were hit by a slump. Production and profits fell as the result of a mass stoppage organised by the Miners' Federation in 1894 in protest against intolerably low wages.

Durham had no desire to reduce his personal expenditure, the number of his horses in training or the subsidies he felt bound to supply to his affectionate, but in some cases feckless, relations. Even though younger brothers and sisters were not over-generously endowed, twelve of them were something of a financial drain on the estate. So in 1896 he decided to sell a long lease of the collieries to that very Joicey for whom he had shown such contempt, and thus secure liquid funds while relieving himself of responsibility for 8,000 miners. The lease comprised fourteen coal mines, eighteen coal-carrying ships, a railway line and its locomotives, shipping berths at Sunderland and no fewer than 1,500 miners' cottages.

For this huge combine he received from Sir James Joicey about £1 million, but retained royalties on the coal mines. At the time of the lease Joicey already controlled thirteen pits he had himself acquired. Much of his business had been gained by keen competition at the Lambtons' expense. Despite Durham's efforts Joicey had succeeded in becoming a Liberal Member of Parliament and had, at Mr. Gladstone's instigation, been created a baronet. In 1906 Sir Henry Campbell-Bannerman went still further and recommended him for a peerage. He was magnanimous and locally popular, but to the Lambtons it was humiliating that their birthright should be sold to the grandson of a lowly employee.

Whatever they felt about his humble origin, the fact was that in three years Joicey, by skilful management, recovered from the Lambton collieries the total purchase price of the lease, proving himself to have been unduly pessimistic when he had declared: "The cream has gone. Only the milk remains." Durham and his inadequate advisers were no match for so shrewd a businessman. The Lambton agent was not, however, an inefficient businessman as far as his personal affairs were concerned. When he died he was found to be worth some £900,000, though how he built up that great fortune was not disclosed.

On Jack Durham's death in 1928 he was succeeded as 4th Earl by his twin brother Freddy, who only survived him by five months. Some of Freddy's descendants demand chapters to themselves. First, however, there are others of Jack Durham's family to be described. Of his four sisters, two followed the example set by "Granny Abercorn" and married into the higher ranks of the peerage, producing in the cases of the Countess of Pembroke and the Duchess of Leeds intelligent and agreeable, but not especially notable children. However, several of their grandchildren inherited that spark of idiosyncrasy typical of the Lambtons.

The Duchess of Leeds wrote one or two books which had no great claim to literary distinction. Her husband was a dedicated yachtsman and Commodore of the Royal Yacht Squadron. Though he was kind and good-natured she thought him a bore and when he died she pulled down Hornby, his castle in Yorkshire, sold his golf-clubs and coronation robes and departed to live on the Italian Riviera.

She had one obsession common to nearly all Lambtons: never to displease servants. At Hornby a new cake was daily laid on the table at tea-time. The Duchess, not in the least disposed to eat it, would cut several slices and throw them into the fire lest the feelings of the still-room maids should be hurt by the return of the uncut cake. This daily manoeuvre, well known in the still room and the servants' hall, was a constant source of merriment below stairs.

A relic of the family's Whig principles was a dislike of ringing bells, even though there was always an army of servants to answer them. Governesses would ring the bell and order a footman to put a new log on the school-room fire; their employers replenished the fire in the drawing room or the library themselves. Lady Ellesmere's exceedingly rich husband even went so far as to saw up all the wood with his own hand and store it, neatly measured, in the wood-shed.

The third daughter, Nelly, married Lord Robert Cecil, subsequently Viscount Cecil of Chelwood, who was a founding father of the League of Nations and at various times a powerful influence in Foreign Affairs. Lord Robert was only a comparatively impecunious younger son of Lord Salisbury and at first Nelly's decision to marry him was frowned upon. However, although she was largely self-educated, her wit, wisdom and intelligence were of great value in Lord Robert's career, stone deaf though she later became. She went from one eccentric family at Lambton to another at Hatfield, but she kept her head firmly screwed on, captivated the Cecil family and like them was sincerely and devoutly religious. The fourth daughter, Lady Anne, did not marry, but devoted her life to the care and support of her brother, Jack, and was the only one of the four to be infected by the racing virus.

It might appear from all this that the fire kindled by Radical Jack had been extinguished. However, the embers were still warm and from time to time they glowed again.

# 5

# The Twin Brother

———————◄►———————

When George, 2nd Earl of Durham, died in 1879 he left Fenton in Northumberland, which he himself had built, to the younger of the twins, Freddy, then twenty-four years old, even though he could not know that the elder, for reasons beyond his control, would never be enabled to produce an heir. Owning the thirty thousand acres at Fenton, Freddy was more generously endowed financially than the rest of his brothers, but in later years, when agricultural prices fell, he was from time to time uncomfortably hard up.

In May, 1879, six months before his father died, he married his second cousin, the delectable Beatrix Bulteel who, being one of thirteen children, was by no means an heiress. His brother Jack was also in love with her and never quite forgave his twin for winning the contest. It was perhaps "on the rebound" that he was later inveigled into marrying Ethel Milner.

The following year Freddy was elected Liberal Member of Parliament for South Durham. He did not stand again in 1885, when Mr. Gladstone's government fell, primarily because of popular indignation at the desertion of General Gordon in Khartoum; but he joined the Liberal Unionists, who were opposed to Home Rule for Ireland, as did his elder brother in the House of Lords. He fought three by-elections unsuccessfully in the Liberal Unionist cause, including one at Berwick-on-Tweed where he was defeated by Sir Edward Grey. Eventually he won South-East Durham, but standing as a Unionist Free Trader in 1910 he lost the seat and after a total of fifteen years in the House of Commons he abandoned politics.

One reason why he made no mark as a politician was that he had a strong preference for the hunting field; but when he was a comparatively new Member of Parliament he did give proof of the Lambton independence of judgment. After listening with mounting disapproval to a speech by his Leader, Mr. Gladstone, he rose from his seat and said to an astonished House: "If the Government won't carry out the wishes of the majority, it would be easy to obtain another Government that will." For a young Liberal M.P. to pass such a verdict on the hallowed Grand Old Man was second only to sacrilege, especially as Mr. Gladstone had been to stay at Fenton with Freddy's father and in an unexpectedly carefree way had romped with the children who were busy chasing rabbits with terriers. Perhaps he wished to divert attention from the luckless rabbits. However that may be, it is not surprising that, although he was personally popular in the House of Commons, Freddy never held office.

Throughout the 1890s and the early years of the twentieth century he was an energetic master of fox-hounds in Northumberland, doubtless at the expense of attendance at Westminster in the winter months. When war broke out in 1914, he had for some years retired from the mastership;

but he took to the saddle again because, although rising sixty, he felt that young officers on leave must not be deprived of a day's hunting as they evidently found chasing foxes a stimulating alternative to shooting Germans. With the assistance of one aged whip he hunted hounds himself, as he had in his previous mastership, and kept the pack going for a full three seasons. According to the Book of Ecclesiastes "there is a time for every purpose under the heaven", and though racing and field sports are not specifically mentioned in the list, the Lambton family clearly thought they should have been.

Freddy's wife, known as Beaty, was calm, sensible and beloved, not only by her children but in due course by her grandchildren, who idolised her, and by numerous admirers in the outside world. Freddy, with the Hamilton good looks added to the Lambton, was as handsome as Jack, and he and Beaty were a singularly attractive couple, though Freddy had his share of the Lambton reticence. He succeeded Jack as 4th Earl of Durham for only five months. He had been a member of the Jockey Club since 1897, but faced by heavy death duties had to sell all his brother's horses as well as Jack's house at Newmarket.

He and Beaty had six children, three boys and three girls, all of whom loved their parents, but were, in early days, something of a financial strain. Luckily the three daughters married immensely rich men.

Of the boys, the heir, Johnny, fought briefly but meritoriously in the First War, was wounded, and then married an exceptionally pretty girl, Diana Farquhar, who died very young and much too soon, leaving him with two small boys. Johnny's brother, Geoffrey, was cheerful, good-looking and popular. He was Sir Alec Douglas-Home's favourite uncle. On September 1st, 1914, serving with the Coldstream Guards during the retreat from Mons, he was killed in a hard-fought rearguard action. His posthumous daughter, Monica, married a Deputy Speaker and being, in the family tradition, devoted to racing, she became the first woman to be elected a member of the Jockey Club. The third son,

Claud, good-looking, good-natured and amusing but with no ambition, lived quietly as a farmer in Northumberland. When he fell in love he was too shy to ask the lady of his choice to marry him and persuaded his even more reticent sister, Joan Joicey, to make the proposal for him.

The first two of Freddy's children were girls. In her youth the elder, Violet, was an attractive tomboy with all the family good looks and a favourite of her Uncle Jack. When she "came out" her daring practical jokes were the talk of London. For instance she painted the seats in Hyde Park so as to watch elegantly dressed ladies sit unsuspectingly on the wet paint. After she married Lord Brackley, good-looking and athletic heir to the immensely rich but reticent Earl of Ellesmere, she became the châtelaine of Bridgewater House, overlooking the Green Park, with its famous collection of pictures of Worsley in Lancashire and later of Mertoun on the Tweed. Conscious of her new responsibilities she let her wildness evaporate, though she was not above throwing coal out of a Bridgewater House window on to the objectionably noisy car of a young man who was paying a visit to Lord Beaverbrook's daughter at Stornoway House across the road. She was too shy to take any part at all in local affairs, which she considered to be a male preserve, or even in charitable organisations, and she shunned any form of publicity. Her impetuosity did on occasions overcome her shyness: for instance she ejected some gatecrashers, including Cecil Beaton's sisters, from a ball at Bridgewater House, an act which infuriated their relations and was for several days a front-page drama in the newspapers.

Violet was vivaciously attractive to men, but always faithful to her husband by whom she had seven children, six daughters and a son. She was at the same time censorious, often hypercritical of others, sometimes inclined to almost hysterical tantrums and no less imperious than Radical Jack, whose reputation she venerated. Indeed, to such an extent did she consider herself a Lambton that she was negligent, and quite often frankly contemptuous, of most of her husband's large family who were only two less in number than the Lambtons, the Greys and the Bulteels. Her children feared and respected her, but felt little genuine affection, whereas a lot of elderly gentlemen, her grandchildren and some of her nephews adored her. She outlived all her younger brothers and sisters and died at the age of ninety-six.

Violet's sister Lilian, pretty as a girl, but an heiress of the Lambton predilection for silence in company (unlike Violet), married Charles, 13th Earl of Home, who was as near to being a saint as any uncanonised human being. Maintaining the symmetrical pattern, she had, like Violet, seven children and she lived for most of the year at the Hirsel, on the banks of the Tweed and only a few miles from the Ellesmeres at Mertoun. Her father and mother, at Fenton, were close by so that there was a family enclave. During her whole married life she never stayed in any private houses apart from her husband's except for one visit to the Ellesmeres.

Five of Lilian's children were boys. They were devoted to her and when some of them got into trouble she was much more tolerant than her sister Violet would have been. Her daughter-in-law, nephews and nieces found her somewhat forbidding aspect, arising from Lambton taciturnity, a little alarming and her habit of examining every inch of them even more so; but nobody could have disliked her. Three of her sons became nationally eminent and so did one of her grandsons. Two of the eminent ones went to prison, for not particularly grave offences, so that the eldest, who rose to the top of the political tree, had the unusual Prime Ministerial distinction of two gaol-bird brothers. This did not disturb him, for they both had delightful personalities, were basically honourable men and were as greatly attached to him as he was to them.

Lilian's husband, Charlie, was Lord Lieutenant of Berwickshire and wholly devoted to the service of his fellow men. He considered that while field sports were enjoyable and birds, beasts, butterflies and flowering shrubs were all worthy of close study, unflagging service to the community was the essential duty of a rich landowner. He owned thousands of acres in Berwickshire as well as a castle and grouse moors in Lanarkshire, but he was as naturally humble as the Lambtons were arrogant. One day in the War a neighbour met him on the road carrying a vast bundle of sticks and logs while behind came his chauffeur-driven car and inside it a poor old woman whom he had insisted on relieving of her heavy burden. He was by birth and possessions a grandee, but he never failed to put his devout Christian convictions into practice and considered pride the first of the seven deadly sins.

If Lady Home was inclined to silence, the youngest sister, Joan, was positively taciturn, as unforthcoming as any of her Lambton uncles. There were compensations which were scarcely Lambtonian. She was an outstanding craftswoman, creating delicate objects with unfailing skill; she played the piano well and was a painter of quality. She was capable of almost every art and craft. Many years younger than her two sisters, she electrified the family, and no doubt in particular her Uncle Jack, by marrying Hugh Joicey, son of the man who had bought the lease of the Lambton collieries and made them once again profitable. She had not been intimate with her sisters because of the age gap, and initially they were horrified by this new relationship with an upstart family which had humbled the pride of the Lambtons. However, as the bridegroom was a man of great goodness and the marriage was both happy and productive, the breach was healed and past bitterness forgotten. Joan and her family also lived within easy motoring distance of the Durham–Ellesmere–Home enclave; and Hugh Joicey owned many race-horses. He was an owner of impeccable integrity; but in those days the Jockey Club was as exclusive as the Royal Squadron and for equally unsound reasons. So the members, despite support for Hugh Joicey from his wife's relations, disgracefully declined to elect him.

Jack's and Freddy's younger brothers had their own idiosyncrasies and distinctions. Several of them deserve description.

# 6

# The Admiral and The Trainer

Next in seniority to Jack and Freddy was Hedworth, born one year after them and fourteen years old when his mother died. By then he was already serving as a naval cadet in a frigate of the Channel Squadron. His rise in the navy was rapid, helped by commissions in two flagships, which brought him to the notice of important admirals, and by his presence, as Flag-Lieutenant to the Commander-in-Chief, Mediterranean, at the bombardment of Alexandria in 1882.

Even in the navy birth and family connections had a marked influence on an officer's career, though many famous Admirals – Fisher, Beatty, Jellicoe – had no such advantages. Hedworth, who did, was appointed naval

Aide-de-Camp (A.D.C) to the Viceroy of Ireland, Lord Spencer, later First Lord of the Admiralty. Then, after he had commanded a sloop in the Mediterranean fleet, followed by command of the lesser Royal Yacht, *Osborne*, and promotion to Captain, Lord Spencer appointed him his naval private secretary. Since Spencer and his successor as First Lord, Lord Goschen, put trust in his judgment he was much involved with senior naval appointments. With the family disdain for what he considered unnecessary courtesies, he sometimes gave offence to officers far senior to him both in rank and age. That is a hazard peculiar to all ministerial private secretaries cherished and protected by their masters, and in Hedworth's case it was increased by an inherited lack of deference. However, influence soon ceases to count unless it is reinforced by professional ability, and Hedworth certainly had that.

In 1897 he was given command of the cruiser *Powerful* on the China Station, and proved that he had prowess in seamanship. After he had been two years in those distant seas, the Boer War broke out and *Powerful* was ordered to Durban. Things were not going well for the British army in South Africa. Ladysmith was under siege and seemed likely to be taken by the Boers. Hedworth called at Mauritius on his way to Durban and entirely on his own initiative embarked a battalion of the South Yorkshire Regiment as a reinforcement for the beleaguered garrison. The Captain of the ship on its way to take *Powerful*'s place on the China Station devised gun-carriages capable of transporting naval guns, and with a battery of these formidable weapons led a naval brigade to Ladysmith, arriving there just in time to silence the Boer artillery and withstand the assault. He stayed till the end of the siege four months later and was described by the General commanding the defence as "the life of the garrison". On his return home he was greeted as a hero.

In those days it was still possible, as it had been in the Peninsular War, for a serving officer to stand for Parliament while remaining in the army or navy, and at the General

Election of 1900 Hedworth was urged by his brother Jack and the Liberal *guru* Lord Rosebery to stand as Liberal candidate at Newcastle. He did and he was defeated, unlike his brother Freddy who was successful at South Durham. But it did give him time to attend to the bloodstock he owned and in which, like all his family, he was greatly interested. Although his younger son's portion was but £800 a year and the pay of a junior naval officer was not generous, that had not deterred him while still a Lieutenant and busy bombarding Alexandria from starting to breed horses in 1882 and having them trained at Pontefract.

After his defeat at Newcastle, he returned to duty and was given command of the larger Royal Yacht, the *Victoria and Albert*, establishing a friendly relationship with the new King, Edward VII, and his son George, Prince of Wales. More demanding professional duties followed. He was promoted Rear-Admiral and became second-in-command to Admiral Lord Charles Beresford, Commander-in-Chief of the Channel Fleet. Lord Charles, Member of Parliament for five different constituencies, was a brother of the King's racing-manager Lord Marcus Beresford. He later became heavily embroiled with the brilliant, peppery and unreliable Admiral Fisher. This naval quarrel split the service from top to bottom. Hedworth was firmly on Beresford's side, as was King George V; Winston Churchill backed Fisher to his ultimate regret.

Having won acclaim in command of the Cruiser division of the Mediterranean Fleet, he was given charge of the China Station. He had a lurid love-affair with the wife of the German Minister to the Chinese Imperial Government and invited her to stay on board his flagship, where she cheerfully settled in. However, he was praised as Commander-in-Chief and when he came home in 1910 fortune smiled on him. He had been elected a member of the Jockey Club and his horses were prospering. There were two excitements even greater than the horses. The first was that he married Mildred, widow of Lord Chelsea. She was a vivacious and amusing lady, whom for reasons best known to themselves the Lambton family called Ponks (behind her back). Hedworth had long been enamoured of her, but divorce was out of the question in Edwardian high society, as unacceptable in the Royal Navy as at Court. In June, 1910, Lord Chelsea conveniently died and a few months later Mildred and Hedworth were married. He thus acquired five stepdaughters with distinctive personalities, to the youngest of whom, Victoria, generally known as Tortor, he was particularly devoted.

The second excitement was that he became a millionaire. It happened thus. Lady Meux, the elderly widow of a rich brewer, was much attracted to handsome young men, and like all his brothers Hedworth was handsome. Thrilled by the episode of the naval guns at the siege of Ladysmith, Lady Meux herself ordered and paid for six naval 12-pounder guns mounted on travelling-carriages and had them shipped to South Africa for use by the army. She lived at Theobald's Park, pronounced Tibbles and built on the site of a great Tudor palace. The entry was through Temple Bar, which had formerly been adorned by the heads of traitors and had been moved to Theobald's from Fleet Street to ease the traffic flow.

Hedworth called on her to express thanks for the guns and to describe his own activities at Ladysmith. She fell for him at once. Each time she met a good-looking young man she made a will in his favour, cancelling that intended for the previous youth. It is alleged, doubtless with exaggeration, that she made fifty wills. After meeting Hedworth who, it was said, even carried her luggage on one occasion when no porter was available, she immediately made a new will leaving her fortune to him; and she died before meeting another handsome young man. So on the sole condition of changing his name from Lambton to Meux he inherited Theobald's Park and the best part of a million pounds, the equivalent of some £30 million eighty years later.

In 1911 Vice-Admiral Sir Hedworth Meux was promoted full Admiral. Shortly afterwards he was appointed Commander-in-Chief at Portsmouth where Admiral of the

Fleet Lord Charles Beresford, newly retired from active service, had found his fifth parliamentary constituency. Hedworth was responsible for the safe transport of the British Expeditionary Force to France in 1914 and he also had the intelligent idea of organising a fleet of yachts and other small vessels to form a life-saving patrol in the Channel.

On account of Prince Louis of Battenberg's German name and descent, public opinion shamefully demanded that he should resign as First Sea Lord, despite his excellent record in the office. It was he as much as Winston Churchill who was responsible for the Fleet being ready and at action stations when war was declared in August, 1914.

When it was clear that the clamour could not be resisted, Winston Churchill, First Lord of the Admiralty, wanted the brilliant but temperamental Lord Fisher to succeed Prince Louis. Fisher had already once been First Sea Lord and it was on his inspiration that the powerful dreadnoughts were built. He was difficult, he was moody, he was dictatorial, and he was unpopular with the majority of senior naval officers. But his personality was dynamic, and Churchill wanted him back.

At the end of October, the First Lord went to Buckingham Palace and put this proposal to the King, who was aghast. He did not think a seventy-three-year-old Admiral should hold the most important office in the Royal Navy, especially in war-time; and being himself a former naval officer, whom the newspapers habitually called "Our Sailor King", he well knew that more than half the navy disliked Fisher profoundly.

The King countered by suggesting Hedworth Meux. According to the note made at the Palace, Churchill declared that he "could never work with him". So the King suggested three other senior admirals whom he preferred to Fisher. Churchill remained adamant, but the King declined to approve Fisher's appointment until he had spoken to Mr. Asquith, the Prime Minister.

Asquith knew nothing about the navy, but he was primed by Churchill whose choice he supported. The King said it was not a matter on which he felt he could over-rule his ministers, but he wished it recorded that he had made a strong protest. Asquith suggested that His Majesty should record "misgivings" rather than "a protest". Whichever word was more appropriate, events proved that the King was right; for Fisher became a thorn in everybody's flesh and particularly in that of Winston Churchill. Perhaps Hedworth was not quite of the calibre to be First Sea Lord, but he would certainly have been a less demonic one than Fisher. Many years later Churchill told Tony Lambton that he wished Hedworth had been appointed Commander-in-Chief, Mediterranean, in place of Sir Berkeley Milne because he believed Hedworth would have prevented the escape of the German warship *Goeben* to the Dardanelles.

Hedworth was made an Admiral of the Fleet, perhaps by way of compensation, and he remained Commander-in-Chief at Portsmouth till 1916. In those days the Royal Navy supplied Admirals of the Fleet with turtle soup. Before that delicacy was commercialised, and the poor turtles therefore became an endangered species, this perquisite may have been more welcome to Hedworth than the increased pay, of which he was in no need. No doubt it was also pleasant to know he would never be placed on the retired list; but it would have been more exciting to be First Sea Lord.

When Lord Charles Beresford, the Member for Portsmouth, was made a peer, Hedworth stood for election in his place, this time as a Conservative. He had no opponent and duly entered the House of Commons where he spoke vigorously on naval affairs. One of his stranger interventions was in a debate on the admission of women as Members of Parliament. He rose in opposition to the proposal, contending that the House of Commons was "not a fit place for any respectable woman to sit in". The House was not impressed by this declaration and the opponents of the motion were routed in the lobby. Women, headed by Lady Astor, flowed or at least trickled in.

He was soon bored by politics and devoted the rest of his life to breeding horses at Theobald's, where Lady Meux had conveniently built a stable, and to winning valuable races at Ascot and elsewhere, including the Manchester November Handicap, the Liverpool Cup and the Chester Vase.

He died in 1929, shortly after his brothers Jack and Freddy, and his widow, living in Grosvenor Square and becoming an entertaining bridge fiend, married the impecunious Lord Charles Montagu. She enabled him to live in the ancestral home at Kimbolton, belonging to his nephew, the Duke of Manchester. The nephew was not only financially insolvent, but in prison. Unfortunately when Lady Charles Montagu died in the Second World War, all the Admiral's letters, and hers too, were consigned to the flames in the confusion of hasty war-time arrangements.

The Meux fortune went to Ian Hedworth Gilmour, son of Hedworth's favourite step-daughter, Tortor. As Ian became an M.P. and at one time a Cabinet Minister, the Lambton influence was indirectly maintained in high political circles, as was its independence of judgment, disdain for toeing lines and parliamentary misogyny.

Next in seniority to Hedworth was Charles, a gallant soldier who rose to be a Brigadier-General. He thought speech best avoided unless he had something to say entirely to the point. Thus when one of his wife's Callander relations came to stay he remained totally silent throughout dinner until his guest had finished a long disquisition about polo. He then said, "Balderdash, Callander," and returned to his pudding. As he had been the reserve in the British international polo team he spoke those solemn words with authority.

As a boy he inadvertently shot one of his father's eyes out, but the paternal wrath seems to have been muted. He then proceeded with his military career. With the Northumberland Fusiliers he took part in Kitchener's campaign against the Mahdi and won the D.S.O. Unlike most of his contemporary officers he believed that loose clothing made for military efficiency. So when his regiment on its way to the Nile marched out of barracks, he ordered his men, accustomed to the bracing Northumbrian climate, to remove their hot tunics. He successfully embarked them all, whereas his Commanding Officer's contingent, with tunics buttoned up to their chins, lost half the men from heat exhaustion on the march to the river bank.

After reaching Khartoum he developed enteric fever and was unceremoniously returned to Cairo in a cattle-truck. However, the Boer War soon broke out and Charles recovered sufficiently to fight in it from start to finish, earning countless medals and clasps and mentions in despatches. He formed a great respect for the Boers who wore sensible clothes and were as good stalkers as any in the Highlands of Scotland.

Fighting and long periods of service in India did little to interfere with the in-built family addiction to racing. Before the turn of the century he rode to victory in the Grand Military Steeplechase at Sandown, proving himself then and on other occasions a gentleman-rider of quality, and later on he acquired a horse called *Trimdon* which twice won the Ascot Gold Cup.

On one or more of his leaves when he was serving in India, he went to Malaya, planted rubber trees near Kuala Lumpur with his own hands and formed the Labu-Cheviot Rubber Company of which he remained chairman till he was ninety. This activity must have seemed curious to the polo-playing, pig-sticking subalterns in his regiment.

When he was fifty-five he married happily and had two children young enough to be his grandchildren. Politics were in the blood, if not in Charles's own. His daughter married a Conservative Chief Whip, Patrick Buchan-Hepburn, later a Cabinet Minister and a Governor General, who was a gifted painter but was in other respects as eccentric as the Lambtons.

After Charles came George, who was certainly unusual. Some judged him the best looking of a notably handsome family and his personal charm captivated all who knew him – grandees, race-horse owners, amateur riders, trainers, jockeys and stable boys.

With one brother in the House of Commons, one in the navy and the two immediately before and after him in the army, the normal Victorian practice might have been for George, the fifth son, to enter the Church and occupy one of the family livings as a not excessively devout hunting parson. He was, indeed, for many years the Churchwarden at Newmarket, but for a career he had more mundane ideas, and in due course his name was better known to the public than that of any of his brothers.

From his earliest days he was devoted to horses. He hunted vigorously with famous packs of hounds, stayed in large country houses, made numerous friends in the sporting world and soon became totally immersed in racing. He took part as an amateur jockey in countless steeplechases and sometimes on the flat. He rode five times in the Grand National, though he never won it, and he was on close terms with all the well-known trainers and jockeys in the country. This slim, immaculately dressed and debonair youth was a familiar sight at every race-meeting. He betted in large sums, far beyond his means which were a younger son's portion of £800 a year. When he won, he usually spent his winnings on buying a horse which he could race himself. He also bought for his more affluent friends, being regarded as a notably fine judge of a horse. When he lost and found himself heavily in debt, his brother Jack could normally be counted on to pay up.

In 1892, riding a temperamental animal at Sandown, he had a serious fall which resulted in his lying on his back for months and being obliged to give up riding in races, though he continued to hunt until extreme old age. So he decided to become a trainer, which most late Victorians thought scarcely a suitable occupation for the son of a peer. However, his eldest brother guaranteed his overdraft and he set up a small training establishment at Newmarket. He was provided with an excellent "head lad" by a friend who was one of the most successful trainers. Various other friends sent horses to his stable and from the start he was successful. His Lambton charm was a major asset, but an even greater one was his ability to know a horse, to treat it as a personal friend and to get the best out of it. He began to train in 1892. By the time he died, in 1945, "the Honourable George", as they called him at Newmarket, was a well-known figure to everybody interested in racing and, through the newspapers, to many who were not.

By a stroke of fortune he made friends with Lord Stanley, whose father, Lord Derby, had held several Cabinet offices and had just returned home after being Governor General of Canada. Father and son decided to revive the family racing stable, which had been dormant for some years, so that the black and white colours, once so celebrated, might reappear on the race-courses. George was invited to buy and train a new string of horses. He might have reflected that Lord Derby, for whom he had the greatest respect, was the son of that "Rupert of Debate", the former Prime Minister, who in his early political life had been a supporter of Radical Jack both on parliamentary reform and on the vexed Irish problems.

Whether or not this was an auspicious omen, the new partnership of owners and trainer was rewarding. Financed by Lord Derby, Stanley House, a large and thoroughly modernised racing stable, was built at Newmarket. Numerous races were won at Liverpool, York, Ascot and Newmarket, and when Lord Derby died in 1908 his son continued the racing stable on a still more lavish scale, breeding horses at several studs. Eventually it seemed that every race-horse in England was descended from one of Lord Derby's horses. Other owners, including the formidable Lord D'Abernon[1], joined the Stanley House Stable and were well satisfied with George's training methods.

The Americans discovered that horses doped with cocaine ran outstandingly well. Some of the American trainers who had established themselves in England made

---

[1] Formerly Sir Edgar Vincent, Governor of the Imperial Ottoman Bank, Financial Adviser to the Egyptian Government and British Ambassador in Berlin after the War.

full use of this discovery, though others detested it. George was convinced that however satisfactory the immediate result, the long-term effect on a horse would be disastrous. So he set his face against doping, but to convince the Jockey Club of the inherent danger, he deliberately doped one of his worst horses. It promptly won a race at Pontefract. He then doped five more which had never shown any form on a race-course. Four of them came in first and one second. His brother Jack disapproved strongly of the experiment and made George promise not to bet on any of his doped horses. However, the Jockey Club duly took notice of the results and doping was declared illegal. It was a major contribution to the fight against corruption.

George's undoped successes continued. Sometimes he had a bad year, with a string of indifferent horses, but in 1910, *Swynford*, which he trained for the new Lord Derby, won the St. Leger. *Steadfast*, a horse entered for the Derby, only came second; but he went on to win eight good races later in the year and became a successful stallion. George was so delighted with *Swynford* that he even added his name to those his elder daughter, Ann, was given at her christening. That was somewhat bewildering because *Swynford* was born a colt.

The First World War disturbed George's racing activities and removed into uniform most of his stable lads. He managed to keep the stable going nevertheless, despite a brief period when the Government, ill-advisedly and to popular indignation, banned race-meetings. He recruited a body of willing volunteers, and he was able to do so because throughout his career he succeeded by his own example in kindling an enthusiastic response in others. His brother, Billy, home from France on leave and paying George a brief visit in August 1915, wrote to Jack Durham: "George's volunteers are a very fine, keen-looking lot of elderly gentlemen." He was much too old to fight himself, but with one brother an Admiral, two of them Generals and the youngest killed in action as a middle-aged subaltern, the nine Lambton brothers were well represented in the field of action. They

Two views of Lambton Castle, built in the Gothic revival fashion high above the River Wear. Today it stands empty, but is maintained in good order and bordered by well-mown lawns, and commands a magnificent view of the large park while remaining screened from the surrounding conurbations.

'Radical Jack,' John George Lambton, an instigator of the great Reform Bill, an influential Governor General of Canada, and first Earl of Durham. (Chapters one, two and three.)

Louisa, daughter of the second Earl Grey (Prime Minister 1830–4), and the second wife of 'Radical Jack.' Her second son, George, succeeded to the Earldom and her daughter, Mary, married the eighth Earl of Elgin, who became Viceroy of India and, like his father-in-law, Governor General of Canada. (Chapters one, two and three.)

Charles Lambton, eldest of the children of 'Radical Jack' and his second wife Louisa. This portrait by Sir Thomas Lawrence is known as 'Master Charles' or 'The Red Boy.' Charles, like so many of his family, was stricken by consumption and died age thirteen in 1831. (Chapter one.)

The children of the second Earl pictured at Montague House in 1894. Standing, from
third Earl), Freddy (the fourth Earl), Hedworth, Charlie, George, Billy. Sitting, from t
(Chapters four, five, six and seven.)

Billy, otherwise Major-General the Hon William Lambton, who in addition to his duties with the British Expeditionary Force in 1914, was chosen by George V to write to him from the front privately and regularly, 'as he did not believe that official communications from the War Office told him the whole story.' Some of the letters are published for the first time in chapter seven.

s, D'Arcy, Claud, Jack (the
lie, Bee, Kitty, Anne.

Violet, the eldest of the fourth Earl's children. She married the heir to the third Earl of Ellesmere, had one son and six daughters and died aged 96 in 1977 having outlived all her younger brothers and sisters. (Chapter five.)

Lilian, second of the fourth Earl's children. 'An heiress of the Lambton predilection for silence in company,' she married the thirteenth Earl of Home, 'as near as being a saint as any human being.' The baby on her knee is her eldest son, Alec, later the fourteenth Earl. (Chapters five and eight.)

Ann (Nancy) Lambton in 1921. The daughter of the second Earl's fifth son, George (above right), one of the great racehorse trainers of his era. He trained Lord Derby's horse Swynford, winner of the St Leger in 1910, and added the name to those Ann was given at her christening, even though Swynford had been born a colt. (Chapter six.)

Hedworth, third son of the second Earl, changed his surname to Meux, as a condition to being left the best part of one million pounds. He ended his career in the Royal Navy as Admiral of the Fleet and Commander-in-Chief, Portsmouth. (Chapter six.)

Lilian's eldest son, now Lord Home of the Hirsel, who as Lord Dunglass had been Parliamentary Private Secretary to Neville Chamberlain, as the fourteenth Earl of Home, Foreign Secretary in Harold Macmillan's administration, and as Sir Alec Douglas-Home, Prime Minister 1963–4, and again Foreign Secretary under Edward Heath. (Chapter nine.)

William Douglas Home, playwright, who during the second world war, took the 'drastic, morally courageous step' of mutiny in the face of the enemy. (Chapter eight.)

Tony, second son of the fifth Earl. As Viscount Lambton, was MP for Berwick-on-Tweed from 1951–73. Disclaimed the Earldom of Durham, but resigned his seat following allegations into his private life which he courageously admitted on television (Chapter ten.)

all agreed that English bloodstock was too valuable to be the victim of anything so irrelevant as a war and so, come what might, George was resolved to keep the stable going.

Lord D'Abernon bred a small chestnut filly called *Diadem*, who became closer and closer to George's heart. She won a war-time 1,000 Guineas and then ran, twice in the same week, in the Derby and the Oaks, coming second in both. As a six-year-old she ran in twelve races, winning seven of them and being second in the other five. Indeed, she won twenty-four of her thirty-nine races and by that time George was so enamoured of her that he added *Diadem* to his second daughter's Christian names.

He was not a man devoted to culture. He had left Eton early, after showing a particular distaste for Latin verses; but he was by no means illiterate. He wrote many articles for the newspapers and later on a book, *Men and Horses I Have Known*, which was justly praised. All the same there was some surprise when in 1908, already renowned as a trainer, he married Cicely Horner, whose mother, Lady Horner, was a leader of the fashionable intellectual set known as The Souls. She and her sister, Lady Jekyll, were women of great intelligence, but dedicated to the arts and learning rather than to horse-racing. However, Lady Horner's daughter was devoted to the arts, to horses and above all to George Lambton.

It is open to question whether George's elder daughter Ann, known as Nancy, owes her first-class intellect more to the Horners or to the Lambtons. She does not have any of Radical Jack's less pleasing characteristics, but she does have his determination, thoroughness and persistence. Moreover, she was an excellent horsewoman who in her youth rode her father's thoroughbreds on the Newmarket gallops as professionally as any of the stable lads.

Whatever genes may have been responsible, Professor Ann Katharine Swynford Lambton, D.Lit., as she may be formally described, became one of the foremost British experts on the Persian language and history. She spent the Second World War attached to the British Legation in

Tehran, witnessing the uprooting of German influence and the banishment of the autocratic Reza Shah Pahlevi, and making a valuable contribution by her knowledge and love of the country. When peace returned she became in due course Professor of Persian at London University after three years as Senior Lecturer at the School of Oriental Studies and five as Reader in Persian at the university. She has mastered several Persian dialects and has written learned books about the country, its language and its history. She was one of the editors of the *Cambridge History of Islam*; and such was her erudition that in 1955, when, after the temperamental Mossadeq (far more difficult to handle than any of her father's horses) fell, the Iranian government was finally persuaded to accept an agreement with the oil companies, and it was Nancy Lambton who went to Tehran to vet the Persian texts on behalf of the Anglo-Iranian Oil Company. She and her father are examples of the variegated and contrasted threads with which the Lambton tapestry has been woven.

Comfortably settled at Newmarket in a house with which Lord Derby provided him, and which he subsequently bought for himself, George won both success and renown as Derby's private trainer in the 1920s, having over thirty of his horses at Stanley House. He also trained those of several other prominent owners. From time to time Lord Derby wanted to be the sole occupant, but financial considerations prevented him, though he was selective in admitting others to his stables.

In 1923 his filly *Tranquil* won the 1,000 Guineas and *Pharos* was second in the Derby. *Tranquil* was a temperamental young lady who had delicate legs. Before a big and testing race it was essential she should have training gallops to strengthen her legs and make her fit; but she was resolutely averse to galloping. Ingenuity was required. George took an umbrella and led *Tranquil* into a large paddock where she remained obdurately still. Standing beside her he opened the umbrella sharply and she was so alarmed that she galloped off. Walking round the paddock he repeated the experiment whenever he came up to her and each time she galloped fast away. A few weeks later she had so far overcome her inhibitions that she galloped to a glorious victory in the St. Leger.

This was a prelude to the great year 1924, in which *Sansovino*, having been first in the Gimcrack Stakes as a two-year-old, won the Derby. It was the first such triumph for the black and white Stanley racing colours in all the many years successive Earls of Derby had entered horses for the most famous of all races. Lord Derby was so overjoyed that he bought a villa near Cannes and called it Sansovino. He also rewarded George handsomely.

Meanwhile, George had had recurring bouts of illness which interfered with his arduous training activities. Cicely valiantly and competently stood in the breach, but that did not always please the far from feminist staff at Stanley House and it annoyed Lord Derby. He suspected Cicely's financial transactions. George had done well financially, backing his best horses heavily both for himself and for Lord Derby who was by no means averse to betting. However, the strain was beginning to tell and in 1926 George and Derby agreed that while he should remain manager of the stables, deciding on both the purchase of yearlings and the entries for races, Frank Butters should take over as trainer. It was not a successful arrangement and three years later George, who felt restored to health, resumed his position as both trainer and manager.

The great slump came in 1931 and Derby was worried about his racing costs, for taxation was enormously increased. In addition to his stables and two expensive political sons, Derby had six houses, four in Britain and two in France. He saw no good reason for cutting down his living expenses substantially and so it was primarily at Stanley House that the reductions were made. He had been top of the lists of winning owners and of successful breeders for several years; but 1930, the year before the economic blizzard struck in Britain, had been an unprofitable season at Stanley House and the two-year-olds did not seem promising. He was angry when in July 1931 there was a stewards' enquiry after his unfancied four-year-old, *Caerleon*, of which Cicely Lambton was one of the few to think highly, won the Eclipse at 25 to 1. He suspected that Cicely had backed it to win, which she probably had, and he was convinced that the Yellow Earl, Lord Lonsdale, whom he greatly disliked and who was the senior steward at the meeting, had deliberately sought to humiliate him by concurring in a stewards' enquiry. He presumably thought there should be one law for him and another for the rest of the racing community. He contemplated announcing that he would never again run a horse at a meeting where Lord Lonsdale was a steward and in his anger he even thought of closing Stanley House on largely imaginary financial grounds.

Wiser counsels prevailed, but he did begin seriously to consider replacing George Lambton, who was over seventy and had again had a serious bout of illness. Also, he had taken strongly against Cicely. However, George had a number of outstanding horses in training for the 1933 season, including the pony-sized colt *Hyperion*. In the early summer, a week or two before Derby Day, George had an accident and felt too unwell even to write letters. So he was unable to go to Epsom and see *Hyperion* win, by six lengths and in record time, a second Derby for his delighted owner. Lord Derby wrote to George saying that none but he could have sent *Hyperion* to the starting gate so perfectly trained. The little horse, with his four white socks, went on to win the St. Leger and George was looking forward to training him as a four-year-old.

These successes did not deter Lord Derby from his resolution to have a younger and healthier trainer. In November 1933, two months after *Hyperion*'s St. Leger victory, he wrote to George terminating his employment as trainer on grounds of health, but proposing a generous pension. It would have been kinder and more tactful to deliver the message orally rather than in a letter, but he was temporarily immobile and in any case he shrank from an unpleasant scene face to face. George was both aghast and furious. There ensued a bitter correspondence between the two men, far the greater bitterness emanating from George, who felt that an old friend, who also happened to be his employer, had destroyed him. He declared that he had only been given six weeks' notice and he declined the financial compensation Derby offered.

He decided to continue as a trainer entirely on his own. With his accumulated racing winnings he bought the oddly named Kremlin House stud at Newmarket. His new venture thrived and by 1940 he had in training forty horses belonging to distinguished owners, whereas at Stanley House Derby only had twenty-seven; and by the time of his death in 1945 "the Honourable George" was reinstated as one of the most prominent trainers in the country.

Meanwhile, the cloud darkening his old friendship with Lord Derby passed away and though both of them were usually too physically incapacitated to meet, they exchanged amiable letters. At least once George was well enough to go and stay with Lord Derby at Knowsley. As he stood in the front hall, gazing out of the window, a rabbit darted across the lawn hotly pursued by two of Derby's terriers. The old butler who was standing nearby said: "Well, sir, if your horses had run half as well as those terriers, you would still be training for His Lordship." It was scarcely a fair comment on *Swynford*, *Sansovino* and *Hyperion*, nor on the fact that of the thousand races which Lord Derby won during his lifetime, the great majority of the winners were trained by George Lambton.

# 7

# The General

———

For the first fifty-four years of his life, the sun shone on William, the sixth son of the 2nd Earl, but when he seemed set to reach the summit of a successful military career a cloud covered the sun's face just at the wrong moment.

Like his elder brothers, Hedworth and Charles, his life in the armed forces began auspiciously. As an officer in the Coldstream Guards he took part in Kitchener's Nile campaign against the Dervishes and was mentioned in despatches. In the Boer War he was wounded, won the D.S.O. and was bedizened with campaign medals and clasps. Then, in the years that Milner and his band of brilliant young men ruled South Africa, Billy, as he was always called, was employed as Military Secretary in the Transvaal and associated with Milner's followers, many of whom had distinguished careers in later life.

By 1910 he was commanding the Coldstream Guards and from 1913 to the outbreak of the European War he was the Quartermaster General at London District. He became a Groom-in-Waiting to King George V, whom he accompanied on a state visit to Paris in the spring of 1914. The King thought well of him, as he did of Jack and Hedworth, and such was Billy's reputation in military circles that in August, 1914, he was promoted to be a Brigadier General and appointed Military Secretary to Sir John French, Commander-in-Chief of the British Expeditionary Force. He was thus at the very centre of the War and in a position of influence.

On August 14th he crossed the Channel with French, grateful for an additional £15,000 which his brother Jack settled on him, in time for the opening salvoes which were by no means as satisfactory as the army and the public had confidently expected. However, he enthused over the morale shown by the Expeditionary Force in the exhausting retreat from Mons. "I think it has been a near thing to disaster", he wrote, "and it is only the good qualities of our infantry which pulled us through. The whole operation has been a mistake, but you cannot blame our staff as they were led to expect French support which never came." He was not impressed by his personal staff who were, he said, "rotten: they are all civilians, old men not much my junior and won't obey orders." Early in September, by then only twenty-five miles east of Paris, after a headlong retreat in debilitating heat, he had to report the death in action of Freddy's second son, Geoffrey, who was shot through the head in a rear-guard action.

The French rallied and under their inspiring Commander-in-Chief, Marshal Joffre, won a decisive battle, "the Miracle of the Marne", which saved Paris. This was the scene at British General Headquarters described by Billy in a letter to his brother Jack Durham on September 8th, 1914:

After retiring for 10 days or more our intention was to go behind the SEINE & refit. The French armies also were to take up a line behind it. Friday night this was stopped & on Saturday Joffre comes round and says he has ordered a general advance and asked us to cooperate. Joffre showed much more animation & fire than I have seen in him before and seemed to think he had got a good thing, said that he was going to put every man in & that the orders were to fight & rout. This is most satisfactory. Well, we remained where we were on the 5th & commenced the advance on the 6th supported on both flanks by the French V Army on our right, VI on our left. The advance has been continued with more or less success each day . . . We have not been very heavily opposed but have had some sharp rear Guard actions & have lost a good many men considering & the German machine guns & Artillery have been very well handled. Yesterday, the 7th, we were crossing the Marne & today are well to the north of it, & have had a very good day getting some 1500 prisoners, some machine guns & wagons. It looks as if the Germans are pressed & it is the first real sight of them really pressed . . . I suppose they will make a stand somewhere, probably about Metz & towards the Luxembourg region. Our men are now full of go & as happy as possible, not that they did not do very well before, but there is much more cheeryness about our advance. The Cavalry say they can do what they like with the Germans, & Infantry tell me they dont think much of their shooting. Our supply arrangements & QMG work have been very well run by Gen. Robertson, the ex-footman. He is a wonder. I am not so satisfied with the General staff which is not quite so efficient & hardly works quite smoothly at times. The flying corps have been wonderful & their reports very accurate; the French General Staff have acknowledged they get more from ours than from their own. Altogether our small army seems to be holding its own well.

At the end of August there began a correspondence with Buckingham Palace which continued regularly for the next three years. The King chose Billy as an unofficial contact with the army, because he was in a key position at G.H.Q. and he was also a member of the Royal Household. So, since the King did not believe that official communications from the War Office told him the whole story, he asked Billy to write to him privately and regularly. He protested that he had been kept in the dark. Accordingly, Billy wrote, usually once a week, long letters giving detailed accounts of troop movements, battles fought, the quality of senior officers and the casualties suffered.

His first letter to the King, written from French's headquarters at Le Cateau, described their arrival in France:

Paris was looking strange, many shops closed, no motor buses and hardly any taxis . . . Joffre was almost in tears over the first captured German Colour which had just come in . . . I am sorry to say the French have been firing freely at our aeroplanes, but luckily up to now with no result.

The anti-German feeling in Britain and in France was so vicious that the King was criticised for visiting and being kind to German prisoners. This arose from a visit to Netley hospital where he and the Queen discovered some wounded Germans, spoke kindly to them and demanded they be treated exactly like British patients. This, the King's Private Secretary, Lord Stamfordham, told Billy, had been turned into a public grievance. In fact, the King, though his only drop of British blood came three hundred years back from the Winter Queen of Bohemia, daughter of King James I, was almost a caricature of the typical Englishman (which was why he was so popular) and he disliked the Germans. Like his father, King Edward VII, he disapproved of his first cousin, the Kaiser. Indeed, he was sometimes a little too outspokenly anti-German, but he was much too kind-hearted to ignore wounded prisoners of war. Billy was asked to contradict any unpleasant rumours that reached the troops. "Psychologists," wrote Lord Stamfordham, "must explain why war stimulates the lying propensities of the mind."

Billy wrote to reassure the King, but the Second Private Secretary, Clive Wigram, said in reply: "The fact remains that the report came from someone on Sir John [French]'s staff – the writer said that the matter should be reported to the Prime Minister. You must have some rum'uns on your staff!"

In Britain there were stories of German atrocities, many of them exaggerated or even invented. However, there were several scandalous incidents when groups of Germans hoisted white flags and then shot down those British soldiers who went out to accept their surrender. They also used "dum-dum" bullets which caused appalling wounds and were forbidden by international agreement. Billy found proof of some of these incidents, including the misuse of a white flag. He told the King: "I have seen a split revolver bullet taken from a German officer, who is to be shot, and there is no doubt some colour for these stories."

Some German subterfuges were clever and not in the least atrocious. Early in November Billy reported to the King: "A German dressed in English staff uniform walked down a lot of trenches saying that all troops in them were to retire. This man eventually aroused suspicion, but he got away. Luckily the troops remained."

When in October arrangements were being made for the appointment of the Prince of Wales as A.D.C. to Sir John French, Billy told the King it was proposed the Prince be attached in turn to the Operations, Intelligence and other administrative branches of G.H.Q. He asked that the Prince be provided "with a good motor car and chauffeur, 2 horses and a groom and one personal servant". One of Sir John's A.D.C.s was to be appointed officer in attendance. None of this appealed at all strongly to the Prince who wanted to join his friends and contemporaries at the scene of action; but Billy, entrusted with his safety, assured the King that he would try to keep him well occupied and as far from shells as possible. He met the Prince at Boulogne just in time to take him to the funeral of the famous old soldier, Field Marshal Lord Roberts, who had died suddenly on a visit to the Front a few days previously. It was a somewhat macabre introduction to the British Expeditionary Force.

On the last day of October, Francis, known as "Pickles", the youngest of the nine Lambton brothers, was killed in action. Though not by training a soldier, he had joined the Blues (The Royal Horse Guards) as a subaltern at the advanced age of forty-three. A German shell burst on the parapet of the trench in which Pickles and his men were waiting about a hundred yards from the advancing enemy. They were buried in earth, but Pickles extricated himself, only to be shot through the head by an accurate German rifleman as he rose to his feet. The Lambton family, already distressed by the death of Freddy's son, Geoffrey, were sunk in gloom. Billy reported that by then the Expeditionary Force had lost three fifths of its officers.

He himself was longing for action. He wrote to Hedworth lamenting the death of many friends and saying:

> Luckily there is not much time to think. I dont care much for modern war. I have masses of office work about twenty miles behind the line in safety and comfort, go out by motor most days to the front, see little and possibly have a shell pitched close to me: was nearly had the other day. They [the Germans] have been very lucky lately and have wounded or killed 1 Div. Commander, 1 Brigadier and about three staff officers by pitching a shell right into their headquarters. What do you think of Fisher? . . . I suppose Winston must have one of his own gang there.

We do not know what the Admiral thought of Fisher; but we can guess.

Billy had described to the King in great detail the retreat from Mons and then the Battle of the Marne, declaring that "the whole situation has made a wonderful change for the better". However, the euphoria was short-lived. What the

111

allied command believed to be a German rear-guard action turned into a major battle, followed by the beginning of that trench warfare which lasted for four years and was an unending misery on the Western Front.

In his long and full accounts to the King of what every formation achieved or failed to achieve, Billy included details such as these:

> The North Yorks were driven back a short way from their trenches two days ago and unluckily were next to the Algerian troops who thought they were Germans and opened fire, causing about forty casualties . . . Joffre has now been asked to place regular French troops immediately on our flanks.

In his next letter, on September 28th, he wrote: "The spirit of the troops continues excellent, and they seem confident in themselves, but are of course anxious to finish off their trench life during which they are subject to constant bombardment." A week later he felt constrained to say: "Joffre is a very cautious commander. He takes no risks & is, I think, depending much on the Russian campaign & so to wear out the enemy. So I fear it is not much good to hope for anything decisive on this side at present."

The arrival of an Indian division on the Western Front was important to the King who, like Queen Victoria, was immensely proud of his Indian Empire. "Some of them the other night," wrote Billy, "crept out and came back with a rifle or two, saying 'they had met some men with rifles – here they are', leaving the fate of the men to the imagination. Others asked to have no wire in front as it would hinder them going forward."

Although fond of Sir John French, he was exasperated by his tactlessness in dealing with Lord Kitchener, the Secretary of State for War, about the employment of Kitchener's new armies, which were beginning to arrive from Britain. The picture of Kitchener, with finger pointed, saying "Your King and country need you", had brought thousands flocking to the Colours, even though as yet there was no conscription.

There was a difference of opinion as to how far the new divisions should merge with the seasoned and experienced formations already in France. Billy told Jack:

Sir J. has not approached the matter with any sort of tact and instead of going straight to K. sent him a memorandum on the subject and at the same time copies to some of the Cabinet, Asquith, Winston etc. Naturally K. has been annoyed and a settlement is made more difficult. I am in despair over Sir J.'s attitude to K., and there are too many politicians of the Winston type and other busybodies who encourage him to go at K. in this roundabout way. He will get the worst of it as K. is far more tricky and can work that sort of business much better. With all his faults I really believe K. has done his best for us out here . . . French at heart is jealous of him and I believe thinks K. wants to come out in command (which I dont believe) . . . I am getting rather sick of the whole business. Why [French] cant leave politics alone and attend to the Army, which badly wants it, I cant make out.

Others were getting rather sick of the whole business too, but Geoffrey Dawson (then called Robinson), the Editor of *The Times* and an old South African colleague of Billy, wrote to say that French was very good with newspaper correspondents while Kitchener habitually snubbed them.

Billy had been specifically invited by the King to comment on the quality of senior officers and on October 27th he wrote: "By far the best corps in fighting value is the 1st, under Haig. They are looking splendid, are full of confidence and extremely well led." It was not until the end of 1915 that French, at heart a cavalry general, was succeeded by Haig. A year later Joffre, too, was replaced in the command of the French armies.

In one of his letters to the King, Billy, who was subtle in interlarding his factual accounts of battles with comments

113

which might trigger action at home, mentioned that a number of ladies, including the Prime Minister's wife, who was always adventurous, Lady Cynthia Asquith and the Duchess of Sutherland, had been visiting G.H.Q. On receipt of this information the King instructed Lord Stamfordham to send a sharp letter to Kitchener at the War Office. It read as follows:

> The King is surprised, and not agreeably so, to learn from Lambton that ladies have been at the Front. His Majesty thought it was quite understood that no ladies were to have passes to go beyond the base and only to go there if they were personally connected with the hospitals. He hopes you may be able to put a stop to these female excursions to the theatre of war: they must cause inconvenience and especially to the doctors, as H.M. understands these lady visitors go to the hospitals merely as sightseers.

They were duly stopped.

The Prince of Wales wished ardently to go into the front line. Billy saw no reason why he should not, but approached the matter delicately. "Up to the present," he told the King, "the Prince has not been allowed in the trenches. Some of them are fairly safe and I wonder whether Your Majesty would object to his visiting one of these? Of course there is always the chance of a shell or a bullet coming, but it is not very great." The King gave his permission and on March 3rd, 1915, the Prince wrote to Billy from the 2nd Division, delighted because he had twice been taken into the front line. He did, he said, get "almost used to seeing the German trenches and real live Boches [Germans] in them, as well as masses of corpses between the two lines. It was fine both mornings so that one was able to use a periscope well." So he asked not to be recalled to G.H.Q. as yet, and when he was allowed a further stay with the 4th Guards Brigade he wrote to ask for yet another two days extension. "I hope you dont mind my writing like this", but he knew there was to be an attack on the following Wednesday. "(Of course anything I should have heard wont get past me, but naturally it is different with you)" and so he felt "it would be nice to be on the spot those two days with the 2nd Div. while it is fighting".

The King was greatly exercised by the ammunition shortage apparent at this stage of the War, but Lord Stamfordham commented that French's strong protests

> do not make matters much smoother. Lord K. sends him all the ammunition available and feels rather hurt that Sir J. should imply he is keeping it back. I really do not think Sir J. realises the difficulties that have to be faced on this side of the Channel . . . It would be much better if Winston stayed at the Admiralty. When he was away last week big questions connected with the Dardanelles had to be settled immediately in his absence. He has no business to be away when important operations are taking place.

Billy shared the prevalent anti-Winston prejudice held not only at Buckingham Palace but by a lot of soldiers and sailors, though not by Sir John French.

A few days later, on March 22nd, 1915, Stamfordham wrote on the King's behalf about the Prince of Wales: "It must be always remembered that *you* are the authority actually responsible to the King for H.R.H., who looks to you as his Commanding Officer and takes his orders from you." As the months went by the Prince proved entirely amenable and Billy did all he could to meet his wishes within the limits prescribed.

Two days after Stamfordham's letter Wigram wrote on royal orders, but on quite a different subject: "The King was surprised to read in all the papers this morning an account (with large headlines) of an interview with Sir John", who appeared to have painted altogether too rosy a picture.

> Such optimistic assurances, His Majesty feels, are apt to undo in this country what everyone with any influence

is endeavouring to do, namely to persuade the masses to take their part in the war and to make them realise the task still to be accomplished . . . the King trusts that you will use your influence to prevent our distinguished Field Marshal from being trapped again.

The Prince of Wales paid a brief visit to the beleaguered King of the Belgians and his army near the North Sea coast. It was then planned to attach him to the First Life Guards as an ordinary subaltern, since Billy felt he was spending too much time with the Grenadiers.

I dont by this mean to crab either the Grenadiers or the Guards, as no better training could be had elsewhere, but I am looking at the bigger point of view. There is no doubt that the Prince's presence at the front has done much good and is greatly appreciated by all ranks, and the more he is seen by them the better both for him and the Army.

It is bewildering that Billy should have thought the Life Guards less socially exclusive than the Grenadiers.

The Prince went home on leave in May 1915. The Cavalry proposal was dropped and there was briefly a plan to send him to serve with the navy, like his younger brother Prince Albert. The King did not approve and the Prince wrote from Buckingham Palace:

Lord Stamfordham's solution that as the King isn't told much about the fleet, he doesn't see why I should know more about it than he, strikes me as being a v. likely one!! However this "entre nous" of course!

We had a delightful week at Windsor really; riding every morning & golf in the afternoon. I saw a good deal of yr. step niece Portia Cadogan who is charming & I had 2 good rounds with her on different afternoons. I expect you find as I do, that when one comes home it is rather nice to be with nice looking women again. I think you'll know what I mean if I've expressed myself badly!!

We motored up here this morning; it was a pity to leave Windsor now we have this lovely weather (for it has been glorious there) but still I have a gt. deal to do here as I have only had 3 days in London since Nov!! Friends to see, gear to sort & put away etc. etc. The King was v. pleased with some war loot I brought back & has collared it all for a collection he is making at Windsor!!

Now as regards my return, tho this doesn't mean I'm tired of home already; far from it!!!! But you said it was'nt much good my returning before the end of the month, so I presume you wont want me back before next Monday, 20th. I can assure you I have plenty to keep me busy till then!! I hear to-night that 7th DIV. has had a scrap; the King read me extracts from Smith D's[1] diary which seems to give a fairly clear account of it all.

We have had Zeppelin scares almost every night at Windsor; it is quite humorous to come home & see all the precautions taken, while we in N. France take no notice of them or Taubes either, tho they buzz over our lines every night!!

In fact the war is taken far more seriously here at home than at the front . . . I hope & suppose all goes well at G.H.Q. I may tell you in strict confidence that they dont think much of Sir John's staff *here*, tho I expect you know that!! I have'nt said a word of course. I only keep my ears open & put 2 & 2 to-gether!!

In May, 1915 the Prince was with the 1st Corps at Béthune, witnessing a massive and costly assault which made no progress.

All three attacks of 1st Div. failed on account of those bloody M.G.s and wire . . . It is all very depressing, particularly as everyone was so full of confidence. Between ourselves rather *too* full of confidence. Of course our casualties are very heavy . . . The sinking of the *Lusitania*

---

[1] General Sir Horace Smith-Dorien.

is a real bad job and is a crowning atrocity; but the brutes did warn us.

Billy, too, had written in his weekly letter to the King: "Our men have been fighting very gallantly and also very bitterly and do not trouble much to take prisoners. The gas stories and the sinking of the *Lusitania* have, I think, fairly roused them up." The Germans had begun using poison gas in the previous month, but by a feat of rapid organisation respirators were issued to the troops in a matter of weeks.

On June 5th, 1915, the King, uneasy at some of the changes in the high command and doubtful of the quality of the British 2nd Army, repeated through Clive Wigram his request to Billy to submit the names of Generals fit to command armies and army corps, colonels fit to be Brigadiers and Brigadiers worthy of divisional commands. "Young active men are required and the old busters should be passed over without any question of seniority," wrote Wigram. "Men of sixty cant stand the strain of heavy fighting. Will you think this over and write to H.M. who wondered what Robertson's views were."

The King, inadequately briefed by the Admiralty, had no intention of being out of touch with the army, a determination which later in the War led him to intervene on behalf of Haig and the Chief of the Imperial General Staff, Sir William Robertson (the former footman, as Billy admiringly described him), against the ill-judged interference of politicians. Billy duly sent the King a list of officers likely to be promoted, but it was now clear that he himself would shortly be given command of a division. "H.M. sighed heavily at the thought of your leaving Sir J. and what the consequences of your useful influence being removed might be," wrote Stamfordham.

In July, 1915, under pressure from Buckingham Palace, representatives of the Government, the War Office and G.H.Q. had a meeting to discuss future policy for the first time since war broke out. The King took the opportunity to impress on Sir William Robertson and Sir Henry Wilson[1] the importance of better cooperation with the French (a subject on which he had spoken anxiously to Billy when he was on leave in London) as well as full harmony between the War Office and G.H.Q. "I hope," wrote Wigram, "you will keep Sir J. up to the mark and prevent him running amok again."

Billy went on leave again in August and after a brief visit to his brother George at Newmarket was invited to Windsor, whence he wrote to Jack Durham: "Very dull court party here: I sat between Queen Mary and Mary Minto and much prefer the former. The King has withdrawn his ban and I am to be allowed a Division very soon . . . it will be a relief to get out in the field and to leave the rather uncongenial society of our staff."

On September 4th he was duly given command of the 4th Division, "south of water-logged Flanders", and received a letter from Sir John French expressing "deep pleasure and gratitude towards you for the time we have spent together in this trying war".

He was not, however, expected to abandon his epistolary relationship with the King or his watch over the Prince of Wales. There was anxiety because the Prince, travelling by car with Lord Cavan, who commanded the Guards Division, ran into a hail of shrapnel and had to take refuge in a communications trench at the front line. The car was riddled with bullet holes and the driver was killed. Billy was informed, with the intention of his impressing on the Prince that if he took risks a lot of other people, especially Lord Cavan, would have their attention diverted from important military duties. The question of the extent to which the heir to the throne must be shielded was a delicate one. He had three healthy younger brothers, the eldest of whom actually took part in the battle of Jutland, but the King and Queen vividly remembered the fate of the French Prince

---

[1] In 1918 Robertson's successor as Chief of the Imperial General Staff. Murdered by two Sinn Feiners outside his house in Eaton Place in 1922.

Imperial killed while serving with the British army in the Zulu War.

The Prince, when tactfully advised by Billy, wrote that he was determined to stay with Lord Cavan and the Guards Division but promised not to cause Cavan trouble or anxiety. In a letter of October 16th, written after an unsuccessful assault on the German lines, he said:

How we all wish we were going south to 3rd Army for the Winter; but we hear we are to remain in this d-d section of the line as I feared wld. be the case. No doubt to be sent round "clearing up" after other DIVS. have made a proper mess of some bit of the line!! That has been the role allotted to us for the last 3 weeks' heavy fighting!!

I fear our gt. offensive as well as that of the French has absolutely fizzled out now with v. little to show for the stupendous no. of casualties; we lost heavily as you know & it took all the original officers & one's friends as usual!! This is becoming a v. serious matter as you may imagine; we are'nt short of officers *actually*, but there are mighty few of the old lot left to keep up Brigade traditions & discipline! It's all *v.* sad!!

But apart from our losses, the general situation seems to me just about as black as it could be!! Our push in the West having utterly failed there is no other alternative than to sit down & dig in for the winter. The Germans have shown us again that they are'nt to be trifled with yet, & the same applies to the French. In Russia the situation is as black as it is in Gallipoli, & heaven only knows what we are'nt in for in the Balkans!!!! I can't make head or tail of what has been going on there, but I dont think many can!!

To return to the part played by Gds. DIV. in the last 3 weeks, we have had 2 absolute "messes" to clear up & have now been given a 3rd . . . We have just relieved 46th DIV. & are having a more complete "mess up" to put right than ever. Of course it was 46th DIV. which attacked on 13th and there are all sorts of ugly yarns going about regarding that show!! No doubt you have already heard them; how I batt. was quite drunk on rum, & wld'nt budge from our own trenches for the assault & if they did, came back to them before ever reaching the German wire!! Who said untrained troops were as good as regulars; God help him now!! I cant help breaking out into strong language for it does make one wild to see all one's friends sacrificed uselessly & unnecessarily which is the case!! Of course as usual the higher command are blamed for the failure of the offensive & apparent waste of lives; but I have no right to say more about this!!

I fear this is a pretty depressing yarn, but I'm always a pessimist as you know & look matters v. straight in the face; well, to do this now cant cheer any one up!! Besides, the reports of the fighting published in the papers make me so sick, being one gt. pack of lies. To read them & believe them, one wld. think we were ½ way to Berlin by now!!

Shortly afterwards Billy wrote to his brother Jack from the headquarters of the 4th Division that all was temporarily quiet on the Western Front.

I go into the trenches two or three times a week just to show myself and try to learn my way about. They are very good and if you care to come out before the bad weather, I can show you such a maze of trenches as will bewilder you. If you do, bring something for your head less conspicuous than that silver mounted cap.

It seems that inviting guests to stay on the Western Front presented no difficulty, provided they were not feminine.

The King decided to visit his army in October, 1915. The Prince of Wales who was ordered to accompany his father wrote to Billy from Buckingham Palace to describe what then happened:

My father was riding an apparently quiet horse belonging to Sir D. Haig. 3 large corps parades had been inspected

& this horse had stood the cheering well. It was the cheering of a detachment of some 50 R.F.C. men that made the horse rear up, & on account of the slippery mud, fall back right on top of my father!!

It was indeed a shock as you may imagine & of course we did'nt know if there were any internal injuries. However we got him back to Aire at once & in bed, tho. he was in pain & as white as a sheet!! Dawson[1] & Bodley turned up about 3.00 & were able to report no complications, thank God, & that my father's condition was satisfactory. But he was suffering from shock & v. badly bruised about the groin; the fall completely "winded" him, & one knows from experience what a long time it takes to recover from this!! But my father was better in the evening & could'nt have been more comfortable than where he was in that nice chateau at AIRE. But he sent me home that night & here I am now with orders to await his return here, which I think will take place tomorrow. But it all depends on the weather. It was such bad luck this accident & in the middle of such a successful trip too.

Billy told Jack Durham: "I think it most culpable not to have given him a quiet or even a doped horse with the whole army to choose from. *My old mare would have been perfect.*" The King appeared to make a good recovery. Indeed Stamfordham wrote on New Year's Eve to say that at Sandringham, where admittedly the pheasants were not stratospheric, he had killed 300 to his own gun two days previously. However, the damage was greater than the doctors diagnosed and the effects of the accident were lasting.

Shortly afterwards Billy received a letter from Lord Stamfordham asking him to propose, as if it was his own idea, that the Prince of Wales should give the Brigade of Guards a rest, especially as they were destined for the murderous

---

[1] Afterwards Lord Dawson of Penn, who was in charge when King George V died in January, 1936.

Ypres salient, and visit Egypt. Stamfordham had made this suggestion to the King, but it had not been smiled upon. Billy did as he was asked. The King remained doubtful, but as the Prince was enthusiastic he finally agreed.

In January, 1916, Billy told Jack that he was "trying to urge on my battalions to do some minor raids, get into the trenches and kill a few Germans. It is not difficult if carefully planned, but you want someone with a stalker's instinct to do it well." The 4th Division was temporarily having a quiet time, apart from sporadic shelling. "The other day one shell actually went in at the door of an estaminet, just as it had been opened at 12 o'clock, and got about 16 men. Very bad luck." He was finding some of his staff irritating. One of his A.D.C.s was "worthy but rather trying. I cant make him hear and have to bellow at him. I find very few people can hear a nice Lambton voice."

Raids on the enemy trenches had always been at night, but in April 1916 Billy organised a successful one by day, believed to be the first daylight raid attempted:

At the place where we made it the trenches are about 70 yards apart so the German can only see from his front line, & the ground on the flanks was also protected more or less by the contouring of the ground. There was one bad place, a gap which was supposed to be held by a machine gun, which we heavily bombarded with howitzers. 2 days before the raid we bombarded the trenches & did no more; on the day of the raid a similar bombardment & then the Infantry marched forward. Complete surprise, no one fired at them & they got into the trenches without opposition. No one was seen for about 10 yds when an officer with both hands in his pockets came out of a dug out, & was at once shot. Then a sentry rang a bell & the Germans assembled & there was a sharp fight in the trenches, but their shooting was very wild. Our men were in in about 10 minutes & claim 2 officers & 13 men killed after which they hurled 200 bombs into deep dug outs full of Germans, which must have done a good deal of damage.

There were two of our parties, separated about 300 yds, & both had much the same experience except that one lot saw no Germans except those in the dug outs at a given time as our parties came out, & we had only one casualty caused I believe by our own shrapnel.

When spring came there was a change and later, in April, 1916, the 4th Division won distinction in heavy fighting north of Arras. The attack went without a hitch, the timing was like clockwork and the Divisional Commander earned much credit.

On May 13th the Prince, back from Egypt, wrote cheerfully to Billy from Windsor Castle. His use of exclamation marks was as great, and as unnecessary, as ever.

My dear General,

Thanks so much for your long & interesting letter, which I received in Italy on my way home from Egypt where I had a very pleasant & peaceful 6 weeks as compared to Flanders, with lovely hot weather naturally!! I was at Ismailia, the G.H.Q., most of the time going out to the front line defences, trenches dug in the desert 8 miles E of & parallel with the Canal. I saw practically the whole line while I was there & most of the troops, particularly the "Anzacs" of whom you must have heard many good yarns!! But they are a stouthearted crowd despite their wild nature & of course the 1st "Anzac" Corps is in France now!! Then I was sent down to Khartoum, but I was only there 3 days & it was all ceremonies & official work, so that I really saw nothing of the country & longed for a private trip up the White Nile!! ... But I was'nt sorry to get back to my work at Ismailia afterwards. I was only 1 night in Cairo but spent another day there before I left & saw the bazzars & climbed the gt. Pyramid as the Americans do!! I only wish I'd had more time there!! Of course I was on Sir A. Murray's[1] staff all the

[1] General Sir A. Murray had been Sir John French's Chief of Staff in 1914.

time, & lived with him at Ismailia; he has'nt changed much!!

I was 4 days in Italy staying with the King at the G.H.Q. at Udine in the N.E. corner. I got a distant view of some trenches on the Corso ridge but otherwise saw nothing of the front & only motored about in the war zone, tho. we did get up into the mountains a bit. Of course to see the trenches one has to climb & it was very disappointing not being able to do this!! But the King is really a charming little man, & very able, & is by merit the 1st man of his country. He leads as simple a life as he could do, tho I got a bit tired of his staff to whom I had to bow & blow hot air all day!! Its nice to be home again for a short time tho. one misses the sun & heat of Egypt where I should have liked to have stayed another month!! I am here till Monday when I hope to get a week in London before returning to Flanders to join Ld. Cavan's (14th Corps) staff. My father is still a bit lame, but is otherwise v. well tho. naturally worried; he rides every morning!!

That was indeed a successful raid that you had; I suppose that is the only way of keeping the Bosch busy!! I shall find many changes when I return what with groups of armies etc. I fear Guards DIV. have been having a real bad time in the Salient; Pa Heyworth will be a gt. loss to the Bde. of Guards, what shocking bad luck getting killed after 1½ years as brigadier!!

The Irish troubles have been v. serious but Gen. Maxwell seems to have done v. well out there; Casement will be shot all right, tho. he'll have to be tried by a civil court. I fear I have no news for you. Sir W. Robertson is here for the week end; it will be nice to see him again for I have a v. gt. admiration for him somehow!!

I sincerely trust I may see you again soon, but I shall be N. of Popperinghe when I get back, which is miles from you. Again many thanks for yr. letter & I remain,

Yrs. very sincerely<br>Edward

Lord Kitchener was drowned on his way to Russia, causing consternation in Britain; the Irish rebellion was causing still more; and in the spring of 1916 the British army was preparing for the great push forward which was to founder on the German barbed-wire defences in the Somme battle-field. The Prince of Wales, at the headquarters of the 14th Corps, was moping in Q branch and having to assist in organising ammunition dumps, traffic routes, petrol-tin water-carriers and railheads. "Alas," he wrote, "I'm still doing Q work, much to my disgust, and am a grocer, not a soldier. This is a foul 'secteur', the Ypres salient . . ."

Billy also heard from Sir William Robertson at the War Office:

The Bosche has his hands very full just now. We never had such a good chance before. I fear L.G. (Lloyd George) is coming here. There is trouble for us. Never mind, that is part of my burden of the war. I dare say I can manage him. I feel K's loss horribly, we were good friends. He was a much maligned man: he was also a great man – bigger than anything left.

Robertson's fears were not fulfilled. Lloyd George did not go to the War Office, but when he became Prime Minister, Robertson did have the utmost difficulty in managing him. His most successful defence was to say: "I've 'eard different." So at least Sir Winston Churchill used to recount.

Billy wrote at length to the King after the great push forward on the Somme had begun and was gratified to learn it was the first detailed account the King had received of the battle. The casualty lists were apocalyptic. Wigram wrote: "I gave the King one to-day of sixty eight pages of officers."

On July 15th, a fortnight after the start of the battle, Sir John French wrote from G.H.Q., Home Forces: "I hear on all sides of the splendid fight your division made and how well and skilfully you led them." The great Somme attack was made at appalling cost and with only modest success, though as before the 4th Division distinguished itself. The subsequent operations were almost equally depressing. Billy told his brother Jack on October 24th:

Net result of two weeks fighting – a gain of about 400 yards on a 400 yard front which has cost me, I suppose, 3000 casualties . . . weather has been rather against us, a good deal of wet, much mist and then some severe cold which have all tried the men as there is no decent place to put them into when they are resting in this devastated region . . . The main cause of failure has been machine-gun fire, every shell hole we make serves as an emplacement for one of these things and it is almost impossible to locate them. They are, too, very well handled and by strong men.

At the end of October, 1916, Clive Wigram expressed the King's thanks for one of many long letters describing the fighting. He went on:

I fancy the Bosche is now staking his all on the war having to finish by next spring. Whether he is right or wrong I am not prepared to predict, but I am sure we shall be severely pressed financially by then and unless we considerably change our mode of life, we cannot possibly continue at the present rate of expenditure. All our Allies expect us to furnish them with everything, and the wealth of England is not inexhaustible.

In the following spring Lloyd George ill-advisedly proposed placing the whole British army, by then considerable in size, under the command of the inept French General Nivelle. Sir Douglas Haig and British G.H.Q. were up in arms, as were the King and the new C.I.G.S., Sir William Robertson, so that eventually this calamitous idea was dropped. Nivelle was a weak and over-confident failure and the French Government finally replaced him with the excellent Marshal Foch, though not before the French armies had mutinied.

Later that summer the mutinies were suppressed with a combination of harsh measures and tact by Marshal Pétain, hero of the battle of Verdun and originator of the immortal "They shall not pass". In the crisis arising from the French mutinies it fell to the British to keep the Germans occupied, which is among the reasons for the murderous battle of Passchendaele.

Before these alarming events Wigram wrote on April 9th, 1917, referring to a number of significant matters:

I was out at the front last month, but did not have time to run up and see you. It was just at the time when the War Cabinet were considering the advisability of placing the whole British Army under Nivelle, but, thank heaven, it did not mature. I found everyone at G.H.Q. much perturbed, and all their efforts for beating the Boche were diverted to defeating these political manoeuvres.

Since I last saw you Uncle Sam has joined us, and his assistance I feel sure will be most welcome. He will buttress us up considerably as regards shipping and finance. If he likes, he can cooperate with us in putting tremendous pressure on neutrals, especially by the control of coal, which has been reaching neutrals, particularly those in South America, for the use of German firms. I do not think that much harm would come if a little more active pressure were placed on the Scandinavian countries. At present they kowtow to any threat from Germany, and are prepared to flaunt [sic] us as they take advantage of our merciful and charitable methods.

You will have read in the papers the exchange of messages between the King and the President. At one time we thought that L.G. was trying to usurp the position of His Majesty and telegraph direct to the President in the name of the Empire. This was rectified before the error was made, but we were done in the eye, as His Majesty's message did not reach the press until after the War Cabinet and Asquith's greetings to America. So long as we have a

128

monarchy, the observances and rules of the constitution must be preserved and maintained.

There is certainly a distinct back-wash wave from Russia rolling over the country, and these strikes and so-called Labour meetings of a decidedly anarchical tendency are the result. I do wish that H.M. would get on the move and show the standard in some of the cities in the north and midlands.

I always have a feeling that the Dominions and Colonies are the greatest asset of the Monarchy and that His Majesty should go out of his way to keep in touch with his Ministers of those portions of the Empire. I was much surprised when the first Imperial War Cabinet met that no message was sent to the King or any reference made to His Majesty. The Imperial War Conference held at the Colonial Office under Walter Long did not forget its obligations to its head.

You have probably heard rumours of the Emperor and Empress of Russia, together with many Grand Dukes, coming to England to find an asylum here. Of course the King has been accused of trying to work this for his royal friends. As a matter of fact His Majesty has been opposed to this proposal from the start, and has begged his Ministers to knock it on the head. I do not expect that these Russian royalties will come, but if they do their presence here will be due to the War Cabinet and not to His Majesty.

Although a digression on this matter has nothing to do with the Lambtons, Wigram's reference to the King's unwillingness to receive the Russian Imperial Family in England is the prologue to an unsolved mystery which is of wider interest.

Liberal and left-wing sentiment in the Western democracies favoured the Russian Revolution in its early stages and the former Russian autocracy was abominated. None foresaw the imposition of an ironclad police state and the massacre of millions in the Ukraine and elsewhere, by comparison with which the Tsarist régime was mild and merciful. In the spring of 1917 the arrival of the Romanovs at Windsor would have caused a loud outcry in Britain.

The King had an affection for his cousin the Tsar, who resembled him closely in appearance; but neither he nor the Queen thought well of another first cousin, the Tsarina, who held her husband in thrall and was the embodiment of autocratic severity. All the same, had the King feared for the Tsar's life, and that of his five children, he would undoubtedly have taken the unpopular course of offering them refuge. There was no such fear while the moderate Prince Lvov and Alexander Kerensky held the reins, however loosely, in Petrograd. Germany had not yet enabled Lenin to return to Russia in a sealed train and the Bolshevik October Revolution was scarcely so much as a gleam on the troubled horizon.

The mystery relates to what happened afterwards. King George V told my mother[1], and Queen Mary told me, that the failure to save the Imperial Family was the fault of Lloyd George. Lord Stamfordham's grandson, Michael Adeane[2], was told the same, presumably by his grandfather. Both the King and the Queen were scrupulously truthful and it seems inconceivable that either of them should have tried to evade their own responsibility by incriminating Lloyd George.

Kenneth Rose, whose *King George V*[3] is a model of good and readable biography, has established to the satisfaction of all competent historians that it was indeed the King himself, rather than Lloyd George, who in the weeks following the Tsar's abdication denied the Imperial Family their chance of immediate escape. As, however, both the King and the Queen continued to blame Lloyd George, Rose suggests that after the Bolsheviks seized power there may have been a plan, possibly involving the Secret Service, to organise an escape from the Tsar's first place of imprisonment, Tobolsk in the Ural mountains. It would presumably

[1] Lady Cynthia Colville.
[2] Lord Adeane, Private Secretary to Queen Elizabeth II.
[3] London, Weidenfeld & Nicolson, 1983.

130

have been through Siberia, which was anti-Bolshevik, or through the Crimea, whence the Dowager Empress and others whose lives were in danger were carried away to safety by the Royal Navy. If Lloyd George finally obstructed such a plan, he must have done so because, probably quite rightly, he judged it impracticable, for once the Russians were effectively out of the War there were no political grounds for sparing their Bolshevik feelings.

This deduction is strengthened by the curious fact that all the papers in the Royal Archives which related to the fate of the Imperial Family have vanished, and those retained in the Foreign Office Archives are only the documents referring to the months immediately following the Revolution when Prince Lvov and Kerensky were still at the helm. The last reference in the Royal Archives is a telegram from Sir George Buchanan, the British Ambassador in Petrograd, sent on December 12th, 1917. In it he said that there was no definite news about the Tsar, but the conditions in which the Imperial Family were living at Tobolsk were "very trying". Sir George added: "It is reported that his Guard has been changed in order to ensure strictness and he is about to be moved to another place of residence." He was not in fact moved to another place of residence, Ekaterinberg, until the following spring, but there the whole family were murdered, perhaps on Lenin's personal orders, in July 1918. It may be that many years ago, in the aftermath of the First World War, the papers referring to a projected escape were consigned to the flames at the request of the Government or the Security Services. The mystery remains unsolved.

The 4th Division's laurels for its part in the 1917 spring offensive, once again at Arras, were recognised by Sir John French, now Viscount French and shortly to be Lord Lieutenant of Ireland and Earl of Ypres. He wrote on May 1st to say: "I congratulate you and your division most heartily on all this splendid work you have done. It appears that you are always in the thick of everything . . ."

However, there were downs as well as ups. On May 3rd
Billy told Jack Durham that he was:

In the middle of a damnable battle which is not going at
all well as far as my Division is concerned nor the one on
the left . . . It has been a disappointing and unsuccessful
day and one which makes one realise how hopelessly
impotent a divisional commander is. One can only go by
reports which are vague, and give directions as to what
you want done. The whole of the rest lies with Company
C.O.s most of whom are, I fear, wounded. I have never
liked this attack nor the way we had to do it. Twice before
the place has been attacked, always with the same result
and yet I am ordered to do it a third time in almost the
same way . . . I fear we have gained but little and had
rather severe casualties.

As he said in a letter to the King, his division had,
between April 9th and the date of his letter (May 17th), 260
officers and 5,200 men as casualties. Casualties usually
included twenty to twenty-five per cent killed.

But war was not everything. In the middle of this desperate
battle Billy wrote:

Is not the stoppage of racing unnecessary? As far as I can
make out it is due to faddists and anti-sports and not
to real shortage . . . we seem to be much upset by the
submarines and to be losing our heads . . . I went to Paris
during my rest (before the battle) and thought I would
satisfy my carnal appetite, but though the lady was quite
nice I found myself useless. I suppose this fighting takes
more out of one than one knows. Anyhow it was a horrid
waste of good money.

On June 24th the Prince of Wales, still addicted to exclamation marks, wrote from the headquarters of XIV Corps,
where preparations were in train for the Passchendaele offensive:

Yes, we are back in our old haunts of last summer &
living in your old H.Q. the Convent! We are frightfully
busy preparing for great things as you know. And I think
we shall do great things with any luck & the French are
relieving the Belgians next to us thank goodness. It's the
1st French Army (1st & 32nd French Corps) & Gen.
Antoine, the G.O.C., seems a nice man & very easy to
work with & full of the offensive spirit!! It will be a
gt. relief when the old Belgians go as they are perfectly
impossible to work with, worse than last year!! I heard
your DIV. had done gt. things at Arras tho. I dont know
where you are now!! It's ages since we last met & I cant
remember when it was; you were in Paris at the same
time as I was in April & I hope you had as good 3 days as
I did!! I was home for a fortnight last month in London
and had a wonderful leave; Portia and Edward[1] got engaged
the night before I left. I've never seen such an epidemic of
engagements as there is: of course Cynthia & Humphrey[2]
were'nt a surprise: it was too obvious before!!

The King comes out here next week, about July 5th I
think, & my mother is coming out too, tho. only to visit
base hospitals so she wont be with him!! I shall be with
the King & so hope I may see you if we come down your
way. Ld. Cavan is very fit tho. he felt last week's heat
rather; but I loved it & it makes one v. fit. I get forward
fairly often tho. they are shelling us a good deal, particularly the back area, DIV. H.Q.'s etc & we are waiting for
our turn here!! Please forgive such a dull yarn but I've no
news!!

Then came disaster. On September 13th, 1917, Billy was
at the front, riding his steady old mare, the one he thought
the King should have been using when he met with his
accident. She put her foot in a hole and broke her fetlock,

[1] Edward, Lord Stanley and the Hon. Portia Cadogan, Hedworth Meux's
step-daughter.
[2] Sir Humphrey de Trafford and the Hon. Cynthia Cadogan.

collapsing and rolling on Billy. His arms and legs were paralysed and his spine was badly injured. It meant the end of his military career. His success as a divisional commander had been such that he was on the verge of being given a corps, and that might perhaps have led to an army command before the War ended.

The Prince of Wales did not forget him. At the end of December he tried to cheer him up with a letter from the Italian front to which XIV Corps had moved. He wrote:

> These wretched Italians dont know the elements of modern warfare with the result that periodically (about once a week) they lose two or three mountains and several thousand men as prisoners, as they cram all their troops into the front line!! Its not the troops, as they generally fight very well when they are fed properly (which they often aren't), but its the higher command, the staffs and officers which are so thoroughly bad!! Thank goodness we have had two or three heavy falls of snow lately so that I dont think the Huns will be able to break through the mountains and on to the Plain for the present; but it is only the snow that is stopping them, not the Italians ... I only got three days leave before going to Italy and after five months without leave I am owed a lot! ... As for Russia, one cant even think about it, let alone talk!!

Mildly consoling though it may have been that the Prince of Wales still liked and respected him, there were few other gleams in the darkness. It was fully three years before he was sufficiently recovered to lead a life even approaching normal. He was never again able to walk without two sticks and he was constantly in pain. They gave him a K.C.B. as a reward for past services, and in 1921 he married Lady Kitty Somerset, daughter of the Duke of St. Albans. He was only fifty-seven. She, already once married, was rising forty-four: so there were no children. Nevertheless, the match was a peaceful and contented one. Billy had plenty of time to hobble on to race-courses and to relax in the sunshine at a villa he and Lady Kitty bought in the south of France. He died three years before the world was once again plunged into war when, as Lord Gort, the gallant Commander of the British Expeditionary Force, rather unfeelingly put it: "It will be nice to see those field grey uniforms again." Billy might have thought so too, for he was a dedicated soldier. The promise of shining military distinction had been blighted for him by a poor horse putting its foot in a hole on the battlefield at a time when everything seemed to be going his way.

# Part Three

# 8

# Branching Out

———————

Lilian, the second daughter of Billy's elder brother, Freddy, was happily married to the 13th Earl of Home. She and her husband had five sons and two daughters, mostly with Lambton characteristics but mellowed, in one or two cases, by the calmer temperament of the Douglas-Homes. The youngest was George who as a boy acquired an expert knowledge of birds. On the declaration of the Second World War, at the age of nineteen, he joined the R.A.F. He went to Canada to train as a pilot and with four others was lost without trace in 1943 during a formation flight over the sea off British Columbia. Edward, the fourth son, was taken prisoner by the Japanese, languished in one of their most abominable prisoner-of-war camps and worked on the infamous Burma Railway; but he survived to inherit his uncle

Claud's farm in Northumberland and be rated one of the best shots in the United Kingdom.

The third son, William, inherited the Lambton looks as well as a good measure of their charm, determination, eccentricity and passion for horse-racing. At Eton, where his contemporaries found him an entertaining wag, they thought he had a future in politics. So, at times, did William; but he was mainly attracted to acting, for which he had a limited talent, and writing plays for which he had a much greater one. He found life at Oxford rather too jolly and was twice sent down. However, he did get a degree, albeit a humble one, and despite an underlying sensitivity he could laugh off adversity. Moreover beneath the bubbling surface he had a serious purpose.

A chance encounter with John Gielgud in the Caledonian Hotel at Edinburgh was the prelude of his having a play produced, though to his fury the producer insisted on changing the last act. He wrote another, *Passing By*, which with an excellent cast had a gratifying reception in the spring of 1940. It was indeed about to move to the West End of London when the German attack on the Western Front intervened.

The outbreak of war did more than disrupt his play-writing plans: it destroyed his equanimity. He disliked the thought of killing anybody or of being killed himself, and he set his gaze on a beneficent, if far distant, régime of international cooperation which would outlaw war for ever. He contemplated being a conscientious objector, but rejected this idea on the grounds that if somebody attacked him he would undoubtedly wish to defend himself. So he joined the Fire Brigade; but there was a shortage of fires and finding it dull he turned to journalism and to travelling abroad on fact-finding missions. This was less dull, reluctant though he was to write bellicose propaganda, and on one occasion in Italy he even found himself flying in a German commercial aircraft with an impeccably courteous Nazi crew. Meanwhile, he decided to fight a by-election.

His call-up papers arrived and he became, like Sir Francis

Doyle's hero in a poem Sir Winston Churchill liked to quote, "A Private of the Buffs". He did not, however, aspire to that ancient hero's epitaph:

> *To-day*, beneath the foeman's frown,
> He stands in Elgin's place,
> Ambassador from Britain's Crown
> And type of all her race.

Indeed, William's aspirations were quite the reverse. There were few more innately undisciplined private soldiers and he had no wish to stand in any Viceroy's place, even if that Viceroy, like Elgin, had been a relation.

However much he might be the despair of drill sergeants and corporals, his intelligence was seen to be above the average and he never failed to be well liked. So "they" decided he should go to Sandhurst and be commissioned as an officer. When he arrived there he found one or two optimistic friends who conspired to turn him into a Grenadier, though others were not so sure. Nothing appalled him more than the prospect of spit, polish and strict discipline inseparable from the Brigade of Guards and when a tentative proposal was made, he rejected it, choosing instead to accept a commission in the Buffs.

His military duties did nothing to alter his conviction that war was detestable and that a compromise peace must be negotiated before the real fighting began. So although appointed Wireless Officer in his battalion, he stood as an Independent in a by-election at Glasgow in April 1942, demanding peace by negotiation. The Glaswegians were moderately impressed and after only three days' campaigning he finished second out of four candidates. This encouraged him to try again at Windsor three months later. After making six or seven speeches a day, he collected 7,000 votes from an electorate dissatisfied with the war-time party truce, but by no means sure what it really wanted. William had spent two years training at the Royal Academy of Dramatic Art and even if that did not make him an outstanding actor, it gave him confidence on political platforms. That, combined with his natural charm, procured votes.

In 1939 he had not been alone in advocating a compromise peace. Lord Halifax and Neville Chamberlain, to both of whom the massacres in the First World War were a vivid memory, hoped for a settlement even after war was declared, if only Hitler personally could be removed from the scene. Unfortunately, the German Führer had the almost solid support of his people, which became more solid still after the defeat of France, and the solution for which the British would-be peace-makers hoped and prayed was a chimeric dream. Any further concessions to the Nazi régime after the seizure of Austria, Czechoslovakia, Danzig, Memel and to clinch it all Poland, would have been totally unacceptable.

William eventually saw that the mirage of a compromise peace had evaporated; but in February 1943 came the Casablanca Conference and the policy of unconditional surrender, initiated by President Roosevelt and endorsed by Winston Churchill (who was William's principal villain). He became obsessed by what he considered the iniquity of this doctrine. Since the War many others have taken the same view and in 1945 even Churchill sought to reverse the policy in the case of Japan. However, our gallant allies, the Russians, would consider nothing else as far as Germany was concerned, and in England and America those old enough to remember the aftermath of 1918 well knew that the Germans alleged their army had not lost the War but had been stabbed in the back by unpatriotic civilians. This time they were determined that peace should be dictated from Berlin and they were convinced that anti-Nazi sentiment in Germany was confined to a small, if courageous, minority of religious zealots and surviving liberals. So, indeed, it was till the prospect of victory began to fade. As for the German Generals, they were as incompetent at plotting as they were competent at fighting. All the same it may be true that towards the end of the War unconditional surrender was too heavy a bludgeon for Germany, even though the Italians had accepted it with their usual insouciance.

William became emotional on the subject. His first thought was to get in to Parliament so that he could denounce the Government's attitude. But he had by now unsuccessfully fought three by-elections and he seemed to be inextricably tied to military duties. He performed them well, but they severely limited his scope. He was a source of affectionate amusement to his brother officers and also to the other ranks who found him neither dictatorial nor supercilious.

His frequent letters home were debonair, entertaining and carefree, even when the regiment moved to France in the summer of 1944 after the start of the Second Front. His boredom at living in a tent, or in a deep hole he dug himself in an orchard as an anti-aircraft precaution, was relieved by spotting birds and writing letters which contained news such as this: "I have been sitting in for the adjutant this afternoon while he is out stealing fruit ... A cow went into [the Commanding Officer's] tent last night and ate his sponge." He spent two months with the British Army of Liberation, during which time he wrote several times to his Commanding Officer seeking permission to resign his commission and rejoin the other ranks. The military authorities paid no attention to such an outrageous proposal in the middle of a campaign.

Early in September 1944, William took a drastic, morally courageous, but it must be said somewhat exhibitionist step. The Buffs and their tanks had been heavily involved in the fighting round Caen, but William was in the reserve battalion. In August they were ordered to assault Havre, the German garrison of which had been by-passed by the British army as it swept eastwards into Belgium. General Eisenhower was short of ports in which to land his supplies. Cherbourg had been gravely damaged, the demands on the Mulberry Harbour at Arromanches were excessive and it was susceptible to storm damage. Dieppe, Boulogne and Calais had to be reactivated and Antwerp was still dominated by German guns. William was horrified and disgusted when the offer of the German commander in beleaguered Havre to evacuate all the French civilians before the battle was rejected by the Allied Command on the grounds that there was not time to do so. So when his battalion was instructed to take part in the assault he calmly refused to obey orders.

This was mutiny in the face of the enemy, an offence for which in the First World War he would probably have been shot. In the event Havre succumbed without loss of life in the actual assault, though there were heavy casualties in an aerial bombardment the night before. William was not to know that and injudicious though his action was, it showed considerable courage. Like his ancestor, Radical Jack, he was ever ready to swim against the tide, but it was war-time and he did not have Radical Jack's secure power-base and popular following. All the same he might well have been comparatively unscathed, for his Commanding Officer and companions in arms were sufficiently fond of him to do their best to cover up his delinquency. However, he could not resist sending to the *Maidenhead Advertiser* an account of his mutiny, based on his objections both to the refusal to evacuate civilians and to the policy of unconditional surrender. He had had his eye on Maidenhead as a potential parliamentary seat which was, no doubt, why he chose such an unlikely medium as the *Maidenhead Advertiser*.

The fat was in the fire, especially when he answered furious letters to the paper with a still stronger justification of his decision, thus repeating his offence. He was court-martialled, cashiered and sentenced to a year's imprisonment with hard labour, a rather lenient sentence in the circumstances. His Commanding Officer, who had generously stood by him, was relieved of his command. This somewhat unfair decision distressed William deeply, but he did at least have the satisfaction of learning that at Calais the Allied Command agreed to the German General's proposal to evacuate the civilians before the town was stormed. Perhaps his gesture had had some effect.

From the end of October, 1944, his address was no longer the British Liberation Army, but Wormwood Scrubs. Letters were restricted and visits even more so. In the intervals of sewing mail-bags and canvas belts, he was able to wade through a lot of improving books and he read the Bible from beginning to end. At much the same time, far away with the Yugoslav Partisans, Captain Randolph Churchill, son of William's *bête noire*, was also deeply absorbed in the Bible which Sir Fitzroy Maclean and Evelyn Waugh had thrust on him as a device to stop him talking. War is an incentive to biblical studies.

With his facility for making friends, William was soon on excellent terms with a number of old lags. When he confided to one of them that he had twice been sent down from Oxford, his fellow inmate replied that he, too, had been sent down at Oxford: "three years from Mr. Justice Charles". On transfer north to Wakefield prison, he found life healthier, for hard labour entailed wood parties, whose task was to move logs on snow-covered hills where the air was like champagne and there were birds to watch and identify. He helped to produce *The Babes in the Wood* as a decidedly unorthodox Christmas pantomime and at Easter he displayed sufficient acting talent at a prison concert to win great applause by performing an exotic Dance of the Seven Mail-Bags.

In May, 1945, shortly before his release was approaching and taking account of remission for good behaviour, he received a visit from Lord and Lady Home, who had from the start never wavered in their conviction that affection took precedence over disapproval. As they were leaving Wakefield prison, Lady Home, sitting in a taxi, saw her husband walking away. When she called to ask where he was going, he replied that he was just going round "to thank the dear little Governor for having William here". Homes could behave as unexpectedly as Lambtons.

William hoped to stand as a Liberal in the 1945 General Election, but not surprisingly the Liberal Party saw no great advantage in sponsoring a candidate about to emerge from

145

Wakefield gaol. He did, however, derive one great advantage from his nine months behind bars. He had the inspiration and the requisite knowledge to write a play about prison life which he called *Now Barabbas*. Perhaps his perusal of the Bible suggested the title. It was an excellent play, admirably produced and acted, and it was received with well-justified acclaim on the London stage. William was thus established as a successful playwright, the career to which (combined with unfaltering dedication to the Turf) he had wished to devote himself before military exigencies intervened.

His output of plays was thenceforward prolific. Many, such as *The Chiltern Hundreds*, *The Reluctant Debutante* and the *Jockey Club Stakes* filled the London theatres. Actors and actresses of high quality gladly accepted the principal roles and William was soon famous. Happily married to an intelligent wife, the father of four children, consistently friendly and no less consistently cherished by his family and his many friends, the rebellious soldier and morally brave gaol-bird transformed his life into a personal success story.

The Homes' second son, Henry, five years older than William, was an entrancing companion, vivacious, enterprising and amusing. Like all his brothers he was fascinated by birds and he was the most knowledgeable of them all. He became a nationally renowned broadcaster, whose talks on the B.B.C. were enjoyed by millions, and he was known as The Birdman. He also painted birds with exceptional skill even on stags' horns cut into napkin rings. When he was twenty-three he married the equally vivacious Lady Margaret Spencer[1] though the wedding bells were all but ringing before she finally decided to marry Henry rather than another seductive beau, Aidan Crawley[2]. They had two sons and a

[1] Daughter of the 6th Earl Spencer and great-aunt of Diana, Princess of Wales.

[2] Later a Member of Parliament, first as Labour and then Conservative; also Chairman of London Weekend Television.

146

daughter. The elder son fell in love with Princess Margaretta of Sweden, but the Swedish royal family disapproved. "Who," said one of Henry's brothers, "do those upstart Bernadottes think they are, daring to turn up their noses at a Douglas-Home?" There was a certain irony in the fact that Radical Jack's maiden speech in 1815 had been a protest against Norway being handed over to the French Marshal Bernadotte, chosen as King by the Swedes in succession to the ancient house of Vasa.

Henry's second son, Charlie, had a meteoric career, rising from Defence Correspondent of *The Times* at the age of twenty-eight to be the paper's Editor when just over forty. He was highly and rightly praised as Editor, and did much to increase the paper's circulation and popularity with the rising generation. However, cancer struck. He struggled gamely to the end, wheeled into his office when he could no longer walk; but he died much too early while on the crest of the wave. St. Paul's Cathedral was crammed to bursting at the memorial service for a man greatly respected for his gallantry and much loved as a human being.

Despite his reputation as a broadcaster, Henry's career was less triumphant than that of his younger son. He smashed his leg against a gate out hunting and was too crippled to take an active part in the War, though he served in Scottish Command. Unlike William he longed to join his friends on the field of battle, and his inability to do so was a source of grief and disappointment. He parted from Lady Margaret and married again twice, being the exception to the rule prevailing until then that Homes and Lambtons are monogamous. He also, which was equally exceptional in two families that are notably abstemious, drank much more than was good for him, doubtless because of the pain and discomfort caused by his smashed leg. He was the guilty party in a motoring accident when under the influence of drink and he was sent to prison. William could not resist sending him advice on prison life. "No need to take a dinner jacket," he explained.

Released from prison after a short sentence, Henry ended

his life in an alcoholic haze, but happily married for the third time. His house was frequented at all times of the day by young and old, entranced by his good nature, sense of humour and knowledge of everything to do with birds; and when he visited the hotel at Kelso, the bar became a salon to which farmers, clergymen, local landowners, men and women of all kinds flocked to be with him and succumbed to his unflagging charm. He left with his friends bright memories of his youth, his attractive personality and broadcasting skill.

The eldest of the Home sons requires a chapter to himself.

# 9

# The Prime Minister

———◄▬►———

It is a dubious but now common practice to record the lives and achievements of eminent men while they are still very much alive. Evidently instant history earns money and delights booksellers. In my case it is an unavoidable lapse of good taste, for it would be unthinkable to describe the Lambton family without including its most notable offshoot since Radical Jack.

The record of Alec Douglas-Home's career, already well chronicled, can with some economy of words be compressed into a few pages. An assessment of his personality is more challenging, especially as it must happily be in the present tense.

Alec was an enthusiastic cricketer who twice played for Eton at Lord's, missed an Oxford "blue" by a hair's breadth and toured the Argentine with an eleven of first-class players. Cricket, like gardening, is generally believed to induce desirable qualities, though since cricket has become increasingly professionalised some of those qualities are elusive. In Alec's case, however, the formula was valid. On returning from the Argentine he thought himself too young just to look after his father's large estates in Berwickshire and Lanarkshire and so, at first a little half-heartedly, he stood for Parliament. Defeated at Coatbridge and Airdrie in 1929, Lord Dunglass, as he then was, stood for South Lanark in 1931 and was among the victors when the National Government under Ramsay MacDonald swept into office on a tidal wave with 554 seats and a record parliamentary majority of 425. With some losses in the 1935 General Election the National Government remained in power for fourteen years.

Chosen as Parliamentary Private Secretary to a number of ministers and finally to the Prime Minister, Neville Chamberlain (whom he accompanied to the Munich meeting with Hitler), he was stricken in 1940 by spinal tuberculosis and had to spend two years lying on his back. In March, 1945, he re-emerged into the limelight with a measured and moderate attack in the House of Commons on the Yalta Agreement. He considered, quite rightly, that the Poles had been thrown to the wolves, but in fact the wolves, or the bear, already had them by the throat and the only fragile chance for them rested in the hope that Stalin would adhere to the promise he had given at Yalta of free and unfettered elections. He had, alas, no intention of so doing.

Alec did not carry this disagreement with the Government to the extent of a vote against them, for he knew the difficulty they faced; and Churchill, who never bore grudges any more than Alec himself did, appointed him Parliamentary Under Secretary at the Foreign Office during the caretaker Government which preceded the 1945 General Election. It was a short interlude and in the deluge that swamped the Tories at the election, Alec lost his Lanark seat. He won it back in 1950, but in 1951 his father died a few months before the Tories were returned to office, so that Lord Dunglass was translated from the Commons to the House of Lords as 14th Earl of Home.

Thenceforward the gradient of his rise was steep: Minister of State for Scotland, Secretary of State for Commonwealth Relations, Foreign Secretary and then, to his own astonishment, Prime Minister. When his Government was defeated in 1964 by a small margin he withdrew of his own free will from the leadership of the Conservative Party, only to become Foreign Secretary once again when Edward Heath, his successor as leader, formed an Administration in 1970.

His solid achievements in these variegated offices were perhaps outstripped by the influence he exerted. Nevertheless, he was generally praised for his initiatives in all the departmental offices he held. He undoubtedly owed part of his success to a determined, tireless and perceptive wife. In 1936, shortly before he joined Neville Chamberlain, he had married Elizabeth Alington in Durham Cathedral. Her father, the Reverend Cyril Alington, had been a celebrated headmaster of Eton when Alec was at school and was afterwards appointed Dean of Durham. Elizabeth's mother was a woman of character with a splendid sense of humour, a typical member of the Lyttelton family from which she came. In and out of office, in sickness and in health, Elizabeth was constantly attentive to her husband's welfare and requirements. Several twentieth-century statesmen have had invaluable wives: none more so than Alec Douglas-Home.

As Parliamentary Private Secretary to Neville Chamberlain he had a vital part to play in the House of Commons; for Chamberlain, though a man of total honesty and integrity with a first-class brain and commendable administrative ability, lacked personal charm for all but the few who knew him well. He made things worse by waging all but open warfare against the Foreign Office, a folly of which I was several times a witness. Under his leadership, some Conservative back-benchers were restive, and it fell to Alec to explain to them the Prime Minister's policy and actions.

151

For a time after Munich (where Chamberlain and Alec each conceived a personal loathing of Hitler) the Prime Minister's position was strong, both in the country and in Parliament; but when in 1939 and the early months of 1940 it began to weaken, those of us who were working at 10 Downing Street regarded Alec as the vital weather-cock and accurate political barometer. We felt that he was more delicately sensitive to the mood of the House than the other politicians with whom we associated.

Chamberlain trusted him implicitly and valued his opinion. I can still visualise Alec, looking unwarlike and untidy in the uniform of the Lanarkshire Yeomanry, setting off with Chamberlain to visit the British Expeditionary Force in France and the Maginot Line, a visit which did much to hasten the fall of the Secretary of State for War, Leslie Hore-Belisha. When Chamberlain sacked Belisha a few weeks later, he did so without Alec being present and handled the matter brusquely with no tact at all.

As Minister of State for Scotland in the early 1950s Alec did much to abate the rising Scottish Nationalist feeling by showing that measures affecting Scotland were being handled in Edinburgh rather than in London. Nationalist agitation gradually subsided and even the Stone of Scone, which had been stolen two years before the Coronation of the Queen, was returned to Westminster Abbey, unfortunately broken in half, but quite easily stuck together again. The practice of blowing up letter-boxes which had E II R on them was also discontinued, and it was resolved that future Kings or Queens should assume the higher of the English or Scottish number. Thus any future King James would be James IX.

In 1955 a new Prime Minister, Anthony Eden, sent Alec to the Commonwealth Relations Office with a seat in the Cabinet. Alec had studied the Durham Report, written by his ancestor, which had been the pattern for independence in the Commonwealth. The time was now ripe for evolutionary change. He concentrated on establishing close personal relationships with the heads of Commonwealth

Governments, with Sir Robert Menzies and Nehru, with Diefenbaker and Lester Pearson in Canada and with Sidney Holland in New Zealand. He travelled throughout the Commonwealth and wherever he went the prestige of Britain soared, even after the Suez episode.

He devoted much thought and time to seeking a solution to the vexed question of the imaginative but unstable union of the two Rhodesias and Nyasaland in a Central African Federation. As in the West Indies, where a similar experiment was tried, failure was due to the refusal of the component parts to collaborate.

While he was Secretary of State the Gold Coast and then Tanganyika were given their independence. The former, changing its name to Ghana, dissipated with feckless extravagance the considerable wealth which had been amassed from cocoa and gold in years of careful colonial administration. Alec thought Kwame Nkrumah a flamboyant and doubtfully sane phenomenon; but he saw the quality, which was indeed almost saintly, of Sir Abubakar Tafawa Balewa, "The Golden Voice of Africa", Prime Minister of a Nigerian Federation which was shortly due for independence. Even then Federation was subsequently challenged by the Ibo tribe, for in Africa tribalism was predominant.

The Suez affair interrupted his labours, but he was led to support Anthony Eden by fear of Russian designs in Egypt and the Middle East. Since the time of Yalta Alec had grown increasingly suspicious of the Soviet Union which replaced Germany as the threat to Western civilisation and world peace. He was convinced that spreading Communism remained the constant though camouflaged aim of the Kremlin. The Nazi cry of "Tomorrow the Whole World" had been taken up, with greater subtlety and less ostentatious vulgarity, by the rulers of Russia. Even when they were cooperative they must be handled warily. The famous Latin tag relating to the Trojan Horse, *timeo Danaos et dona ferentes* – I fear the Greeks, even when they bring gifts – was frequently applicable in the twentieth century.

In 1960 Harold Macmillan appointed Alec Foreign

Secretary. Despite immediate criticism of the appointment of a peer to the Foreign Office (which had neither greeted Lord Halifax in 1938 nor was to greet Lord Carrington in later years), his three years' tenure of the office was in the event widely applauded. Membership of the House of Lords gave him time to travel and he wisely took Elizabeth with him on most of his journeys, which included visits to the great international figures of the period: Adenauer, de Gaulle and President Kennedy. He even invited Mr. Gromyko, who outclassed the Lambtons in taciturnity, to lunch in that temple of Conservatism, the Carlton Club. He had to cope with grave problems in Cyprus, with Britain's attitude to the Vietnam War and with wearisome confrontations at the United Nations or in Geneva. In none of these meetings or conferences did he put a foot wrong and the Foreign Office officials thought him the ideal Foreign Secretary, although he was far from being a mere cipher in the making of policy.

On the eve of the Conservative Party Conference in 1963, Harold Macmillan was stricken by an illness which seemed graver at the time than it subsequently proved. He decided to resign. The main contenders in the race to succeed were R. A. Butler, who had been the favourite in 1957, Lord Hailsham and Mr. Reginald Maudling. The betting was on Hailsham, for Macmillan disliked Butler, for all his great qualities. There was no obligation on the Queen to ask the opinion of the outgoing Prime Minister. She had not done so in 1955 when Churchill resigned or in January, 1957, when Eden went. However, it seemed probable that in this case she would do so; and she did.

Nobody was thinking of Lord Home as Harold Macmillan's successor, least of all Lord Home himself. It was inconceivable that a peer should be Prime Minister; but by a quirk of fortune earlier that year Parliament, in approving a Bill to allow those who succeeded to peerages to renounce them (a measure largely designed to meet the wishes of the Hon. Anthony Wedgwood Benn), had also allowed existing hereditary peers one year in which they might renounce. This was primarily to please Lord Hailsham, but it also covered Lord Home and, at a later date, Lord Lambton.

The matter was settled in perhaps too great a hurry for the health of the Conservative Party. The pressure of the Party Conference and the avid interest of the newspapers contributed to the speed with which a decision was taken; but there can be no doubt that the choice was primarily Harold Macmillan's. When the Queen, having consulted Macmillan in his nursing home, sent for Alec, I was less surprised than most people. As long ago as 1939 a lady of long political experience at 10 Downing Street had assured me – as I had recorded in my diary[1] – that Lord Dunglass would one day be Prime Minister; but I had a more recent and more cogent reason for thinking it possible.

In November, 1961 I was dining at the Other Club, Winston Churchill's personally conducted dining club. R. A. Butler was in the Chair and others present included Churchill and Macmillan. Sir Norman Brook, Secretary to the Cabinet, was also dining and Alec Home had just been elected a member of the club. In the course of conversation I asked Brook what would happen if some ill befell Harold Macmillan. He replied that the right man to succeed would be Alec Home: "I think he is the only one who would do it well."

The Secretary to the Cabinet is always powerful, and Norman Brook was the most powerful of them all. Churchill and Eden had constantly sought his advice, even on political appointments, and Harold Macmillan followed in their footsteps. It is probable that in making his recommendation to the Queen, Macmillan, who in any event thought highly of the Foreign Secretary, had in mind the advice of Norman Brook, even though Brook had retired from the public service nine months previously. That, at any rate, was the two and two which, rightly or wrongly, I put together on hearing that the Queen had sent for Alec.

He was both astonished and reluctant, and since Ian Macleod and Enoch Powell made it clear they would not

---

[1] *The Fringes of Power* (London, Hodder and Stoughton, 1985).

serve in his Cabinet, he was not sure he could form a durable Administration. However, the Tory elders urged him to accept and R. A. Butler, with unselfseeking loyalty, was joined by the two other main contestants, Hailsham and Maudling, in pledging support.

The reactions of his nearest and dearest were predictably Lambtonian. His mother, who usually voted Labour (as, in 1945, did her aunt, Lady Robert Cecil), told the television journalists that he had been a very ordinary little boy and said she had hoped the choice would fall on Mr. Butler; his brother, Edward, filmed emerging from some reeds with a gun and a dead duck, gave emphasis to the "grouse-moor image" which the Labour Party were seeking to foster; William told a somewhat embarrassing story about his brother; Alec's aunt, Lady Ellesmere, said she thought it an *extraordinary* choice; and his uncle, Lord Durham, said it was "a disaster".

For one week a peer was Prime Minister of the United Kingdom in the 1960s, for it took Alec that amount of time to renounce his peerage and be offered a seat in Scotland which he could contest in a by-election. The hero who made the sacrifice, George Younger, did not suffer in the long run, for many years later he was Secretary of State for Scotland and then Minister of Defence. Alec's own comment on this drama is as follows: "Although the procedures had been well tested, I determined to change them so that anyone who followed me should be spared the public vivisection to which I was exposed. Anyhow, although I liked Rab a lot I don't think he would have made a good P.M." Winston Churchill, Lord Waverley and Lord Chandos, all of whom liked Rab a lot, had come to the same conclusion in January, 1957, when Anthony Eden resigned. So had a large majority of the Cabinet.

Alec's term as Prime Minister was the shortest since George Canning's and Lord Goderich's brief Administration in the 1820s and it had to be largely devoted to winning the forthcoming General Election. When Anthony Eden wanted Churchill to retire in 1954, a year before a General Election,

Churchill reminded him of Rosebery after Gladstone, of Balfour after Salisbury. Both held office for a short time and lost the subsequent election, though Rosebery won the Derby during his brief tenure. To those two infelicitous examples now had to be added Home after Macmillan.

The 1964 General Election campaign did not show Alec at his best. He was unpractised in the art of television, which was a new arrival on the electoral scene, and he had recently made a joke which misfired by confessing to a journalist that he was a poor mathematician who did his sums with matchsticks. The Labour leader, Harold Wilson, made public fun of this and, in an effort to stir up class feeling, poured scorn on the 14th Earl of Home. Alec scored a point by saying that Harold Wilson was also presumably the 14th Mr. Wilson. The Labour Party played a number of dirty tricks, winning the anti-nuclear vote by promising to abolish the Polaris submarines, which they had no intention of doing, and organising rabbles to shout down Alec whenever he made a speech. Only a year before Macmillan resigned, the electors of Orpington, the archetype of a safe Conservative seat, had shown they were disenchanted with the Government by returning a Liberal in a by-election; and there had been other electoral disasters. It was a menacing omen.

Despite all this the Government only lost the election by four seats and the combined Conservative and Liberal votes exceeded those of the Labour Party, as indeed they did again in 1966. Some concluded that if R. A. Butler had been Prime Minister in 1964 the Tories would have won, others that it was only Alec's transparent honesty and charisma that averted the far more dramatic loss of seats they suffered two years later. No one can tell which view is correct, but after thirteen years of Tory rule, popular and successful though, except for Suez, that had been, the floating voters who decide election results wanted a change.

Alec took his narrow defeat philosophically. He was criticised and he decided that in the aftermath it would be right to surrender the leadership of the Conservative Party. In the ensuing contest for the succession Ted Heath defeated Maudling. Alec, with no recrimination, gave unwavering loyalty to the new leader, becoming Foreign Secretary for the second time when Heath won the 1970 election. Tirelessly he set forth on his travels again, including a visit to China where Chou-en-Lai was a friendly and forthcoming host who even arranged for the Eton Boating Song to be played at a government banquet. At home Britain at last entered the Common Market and Alec fought hard, though finally without success, both to negotiate a settlement with Ian Smith in Rhodesia and to unravel the hideous tangles in the Middle East. He also expelled from Britain a hundred and five spies masquerading as Soviet diplomats.

The Conservatives lost the 1974 election, which followed a miners' strike that the Government handled ineptly. Vic Feather, the moderate and sensible General Secretary of the Trades Unions Congress, told me that the T.U.C. went to Downing Street anxious to help settle the matter, but they were estranged by Ted Heath's uncompromising attitude and left No. 10 in a mood quite different from that in which they had arrived. The subsequent decision of the electorate enabled the trade union leaders to dictate to the new Labour Government, which they did unhindered for the next five years until financial stringency necessitated a change of course.

However that may be, Alec's political career was over; but well into his eighties he has continued to be an active participant in House of Lords' debates and is in constant demand as a speaker, after dinner, in the pulpit and at meetings or conferences. Few elder statesmen have been held in greater respect or have spent so bright an evening of their lives, unhindered by any sign of failing physical powers. He even finds time for the hereditary addiction to horse-racing.

So much for a summarised account of Alec Home's career and achievements. His personality requires more careful exposition. The cross-breeding of Home and Lambton would enliven any stud-book.

Perhaps in Alec, unlike his brothers and sisters, the Home strain is the stronger, though the sharpness of wit is certainly Lambton. In place of reticence Alec displays calmness – calmness in political crisis, in prosperity and in adversity. Nobody claims to have seen him rattled; and if ever he has been it can only have been on a cricket pitch or when a favourite azalea wilted.

Courage nearly always accompanies calmness and so, in Alec's case, does simplicity, which is the most endearing of virtues. It is not a common quality and it is one which eschews vanity, for men of true simplicity are instinctively humble. It eluded Radical Jack altogether. As Bismarck once said to Queen Victoria's daughter, the Empress Frederick: "A man is only worth what remains of him when you subtract his personal vanity from the rest." Leading politicians tend to be vain, and of twentieth-century Prime Ministers Alec Home is matched only by Clement Attlee, and perhaps Sir Henry Campbell-Bannerman, in a total absence of vanity, though in Churchill's case self-assurance replaced it and Lady Churchill, like Elizabeth Home, was often worried by her husband's carelessness of dress and appearance. She wished he were a little more personally vain.

Alec has two characteristics which are not typical of Lambtons. One is a love of everything to do with nature: birds, beasts, butterflies, and flowers. Indeed, though none could say that he is anything but masculine, he has a gift for arranging flowers which is more often a feminine attribute, and when he was prostrate on his back he embroidered eight chair seats. Like his brothers he knows a lot about birds, and for all varieties preservation, study and admiration are ardent Home pursuits, foreign to Lambtons.

His second distinctive characteristic is a deeply felt and firmly held religious faith by no means common to all Lambtons. For most of them going to church was a weekly exercise simply because before 1914 not to attend Matins at 11 a.m. on a Sunday morning would have been worse than eccentric. The General, Sir William, obviously surprised his brother Jack when he wrote from the headquarters of the 4th Division in France, "I have taken to Church going from a sense of duty and quite like it." His sister, Lady Robert Cecil, did, however, have a sincere faith which she demonstrated in her life and which was a source of much satisfaction to the devout Cecil family. There were one or two others, notably General Charles and George, who did not flaunt their religion, but were by no means immune to faith.

Alec's father was a devout Christian who did all he could to live in accordance with the faith he professed. Alec, after long and protracted contemplation, followed his father's example, though regular attendance at divine service is difficult for a perambulating Secretary of State. In his short autobiography[1] he included a declaration of faith based on his conviction "that the complex ordering of nature which included man could not be the work of chance". He rang many concordant bells when he said: "I believe that men have made unbelievably heavy weather of the message of Christ."

A proof of Alec's Christian faith is found in his total lack of spite or rancour. He showed this throughout his political career, but most clearly in bearing no ill-will towards Ted Heath, his successor as leader of the Conservative Party. Chamberlain showed comparable humility when he took office under his successor, Winston Churchill; but that was at a critical time in the War, and a lesser man than Alec would have resented his supersession by Heath, as Heath regrettably did when he in turn was ousted to make room for Margaret Thatcher. Rancour and asperity are traditionally thought permissible in party politics, but outside the Houses of Parliament Alec found them detestable.

Few traditions are more harmful to the good of the country than the belief that it is always the duty of the Opposition to oppose. In disputes over party policy that must be so, but it should be the duty of the Opposition to support any measure which is in the national interest. This was the case

[1] *The Way the Wind Blows* (London, Collins, 1976)

when Churchill and Attlee, Eden and Bevin, saw eye to eye on foreign policy, and when Butler and Gaitskell agreed on much that they believed to be for the common good. Now, particularly in the 1970s and 80s, professional politicians, sometimes of pygmy stature, seem to believe that the interests of the party are more important than the interests of the state and that it is sound political doctrine to preach compassion while practising spite. Alec would have none of this. For him the national interest came first, even when achieving it lay in the hands of the opposite party and success would be likely to benefit them electorally.

Although always ready to listen to others (for he never has anything but perfect good manners) Alec, like his brother William, has inherited the Lambton independence of judgment. He combines it with a more than average quota of commonsense. Loyalty, which is natural to him, does not imply subservience to the herd, and he has always walked in what he himself judges to be the straight and narrow way. Although immersed in politics, he was never truly a professional politician, for he would have sacrificed office to principle, had the occasion arisen, and would always, like Cincinnatus, have been willing to return to the plough. Lord Salisbury, who had many comparable characteristics, finally did so and had indeed considered resignation on several previous occasions. Of course, it is an advantage to have broad acres to which to return and not to be dependent on a ministerial salary; but it is a misfortune when politicians, for financial reasons, feel bound to continue treading a path which in their hearts they find antipathetic.

Alec has always been gentle, disliking unseemly disputes and anxious to see the best in others. This is one reason why he has never failed to get on with those who worked for him, with his colleagues and even with his political opponents. By charm of manner he bewitched Commonwealth leaders and foreign statesmen, and he disarmed not only his 1964 antagonist, Harold Wilson, but also Chou-en-Lai, General de Gaulle, Henry Kissinger and the inscrutable Gromyko.

161

He would not claim to be an intellectual, but he is fully capable of original thought. He may not have been, at any rate in his prime-ministerial days, effective on television, but as a speaker on serious matters, as well as on lighter themes, he is a master of wit, and as long as he lives he will be relentlessly sought after to satisfy an audience. Still, in his eighties, an active participant in both sport and current affairs, he has proved himself a man for a number of surprisingly different seasons. Perhaps he inherits that from Radical Jack.

# 10

# Tony

When Freddy, 4th Earl of Durham, died a few months after his brother Jack, his eldest son, Johnny, inherited Lambton and Fenton with a great many thousand acres and the diminished, but still substantial remnant of the great Durham fortune. In the War he had fought with the Northumberland Fusiliers, part of a Northumbrian division which had been sent into the line inadequately trained only three days after landing in France. He was badly wounded, an injury which impeded martial, but not marital, activities.

A year after the Great War ended he married the lovely eighteen-year-old Diana Farquhar with whom he was passionately in love. Diana's father was Granville Farquhar, who was intelligent, had made a fortune in the City, rode well to hounds but was primarily renowned for his black temper. On one occasion, when staying at Fenton, he flew into a rage for no good reason at all and shot two of the swans on the lake. He said they were eating the fish, which is not a vice usually ascribed to swans. Diana died in 1924 of septic pneumonia just after her twenty-third birthday, leaving her unhappy husband with two small boys. For a long time he was inconsolable.

He spoilt his two sons, Roddy and Tony, but provided them with no guidance. They were allowed to run wild and never punished, whatever their extravagances. Johnny himself, always pleasant and friendly, had none of the Lambton acerbity and was physically attractive. He had a good brain which he preferred not to use, and he developed into a charming, cultivated but lazy dilettante. As well as horses and books, he liked good claret. He laid down many dozen bottles of the best. Unfortunately, his otherwise impeccable butler surreptitiously consumed them almost as fast as he bought them. As an eligible widower several ladies cast hopeful eyes on him. His choice eventually fell on a likeable and good-natured racing enthusiast, Hermione Bullough, who was also a great heiress. Step-mothers have a testing task and both Roddy and Tony presented problems with which she found it difficult to cope, though she tried her best.

Roddy inherited his grandfather's bad temper. He was sent to Harrow where, though adequately endowed with intelligence, he was totally undistinguished. He was jealous of his younger brother who shot and played cricket better than he did, and as the years went by the two boys drifted far apart. In February, 1941, faced with the uncongenial obligation to serve in the army, Roddy felt insecure and unhappy. Indeed he was the prototype of the "angry young man" of two decades later. He went to the extreme length of blowing his brains out in the middle of the night on the frozen fountain at Fenton, dyeing the snow crimson with his blood. The next morning Tony, who had once worshipped him, looked out of the window on the appalling scene. He was overcome with horror, but as time went by what principally worried him was that he had not tried harder to influence his brother on to a less disastrous path. Everybody was shocked: but Roddy's family had not found him, handsome though he was, a lovable young man.

Materially, Tony lacked for nothing. In the holidays he was provided with plenty of shooting (at which he excelled), fishing and other diversions. What he lacked was affection. His grandmother, the admirable Beaty, could have provided it, but she had many other grandchildren, twenty in all, to share her attention, and she died when Tony was fifteen. The absence of parental direction was a grave deprivation. His father was too easy-going to supply it and thought that giving in to his children's demands was an acceptable substitute.

From his early teens Tony was dogged by bouts of ill health. At Harrow he seldom spent more than one whole term at school in any year and he had to be "off games". This offered one advantage, for he could sit in his room and read. Before leaving Harrow he devoured the whole of Dickens and Thackeray, most of Sir Walter Scott and much other improving literature. He also learned to write English well. He was, like his brother, both good-looking and capable of tempestuous rage; but like Radical Jack the bouts of anger were short-lived and there were no grudges.

When war broke out in 1939 he was seventeen. He enlisted in the army and was sent to Sandhurst; but he was stricken by severe jaundice accompanied by eye trouble. It was sufficiently serious for him to be invalided out of the army and he spent the rest of the War working in an armaments factory at Newcastle and later at an agricultural college. Jaundice was an affliction which together with pneumonia recurred from time to time during the next thirty-five years and made a severe impact, psychologically as well as physically. His liver was damaged, his self-confidence was shaken, his sensitivity sharpened.

None of this affected his appeal to the other sex. When he was twenty he met and married a pretty girl of nineteen called Belinda Blew-Jones, who has an original mind. By her in course of time he had five daughters and a son, thus falling only one short of the Ellesmere and Home scores. Belinda was engaged when they met, but so powerful was Tony's attraction that she broke off her engagement and married him. Johnny gave them Biddick, a beautiful Queen Anne manor house near Lambton Castle. He later made over the rest of the estate, in ample time to avoid death duties, and retired to live happily in Sussex with his wife Hermione and go to race-meetings.

In the 1945 General Election Tony contested Chester-le-Street, close to Lambton Castle. He did so in the Conservative cause, for the traditional Liberal mantle of the Lambtons had been discarded. The constituency, largely inhabited by miners whose grandparents had worked in the Lambton collieries, could never have fallen to the Conservatives even if there had been a landslide in their favour rather than, as happened in 1945, in the opposite direction. The Labour candidate was Jack Lawson, a wise and justly esteemed representative of the old Labour Party at its best. His canvassers called Tony "The Lambton Worm", a name given in mediaeval times to a monstrous reptile believed to inhabit the River Wear and devour all the farmers' livestock. When the election was over Lawson, newly appointed Secretary of State for War, came to Chequers and in the course of conversation at luncheon told Mr. Attlee about the Lambton Worm stratagem. He added that he had been greatly impressed by young Lambton's courage and ability in fighting a hopeless battle. He prophesied that one day Tony would go far in politics. But for certain developments he might have been right.

While awaiting a further political opening, he began to write articles for the newspapers, mainly, at a later stage, for the Beaverbrook press. Lord Beaverbrook was impressed by his journalistic talent and found his company stimulating. He also shared Tony's liking for the macabre.

By the time of the 1951 General Election the name of Viscount Lambton was well known, not least in the north where his family had been so prominent for centuries. He stood for the Liberal stronghold of Berwick-on-Tweed, that city which is neither in England nor in Scotland and is alleged, due to an oversight by the Foreign Office after the Crimean War, to be still at war with the Russian Empire. His grandfather had failed to win the seat in a contest with Sir Edward Grey, but Tony won it and remained its Member of Parliament for twenty-two years. On his leaving the political scene the Liberals won it back to its traditional allegiance.

In the House of Commons he made friends with Selwyn Lloyd, Minister of State at the Foreign Office, who on succeeding Harold Macmillan as Foreign Secretary in December 1955 invited Tony to be his Parliamentary Private Secretary. He was attentive to his duties in the House and developed an unshakeable loyalty to Lloyd. A year later he developed an equal and opposite disloyalty to Harold Macmillan whom he considered primarily responsible for the Suez débâcle. This feeling was exacerbated when in 1962 Macmillan unceremoniously discarded Selwyn Lloyd, then Chancellor of the Exchequer, together with a third of the whole Cabinet in what was called The Night of the Long Knives. Thenceforward Tony never ceased to drive his own long knife into Macmillan, in speech and in writing, whenever he could find an opportunity. They even had an unseemly dispute on the steps of Westminster Cathedral after the memorial service for President Kennedy. Like his ancestors he preferred principle to preferment.

It was thirteen years before he held office, so that he had plenty of time for other occupations. He wrote weekly articles for the *Evening Standard*, often astringent, sometimes a little too daringly outspoken, but applauded by Lord Beaverbrook while he lived and by the paper's readers. He invested shrewdly, increasing his wealth and improving his property; and he sold fifteen hundred acres for the construction of a new town at Washington (in County Durham, not in the District of Columbia). At Lambton he created the biggest pheasant shoot in the kingdom. Though not consistently addicted to racing, he owned a horse called *Jupiter* which won the Cambridgeshire, with Gordon Richards up, and thereafter he always kept one horse in training.

Nor did he neglect his duties in his constituency, where he was both liked and respected, or in the House of Commons. He sponsored an Obscene Publications Bill, which proposed making the test of obscenity an author's intention; he urged the reintroduction of some form of National Service; and in 1969 he tried to win support for a Bill of Rights to guarantee the freedom of the individual, a proposal which would have had substantial support, but which Harold Wilson's Government opposed and defeated. He made sharp criticisms of the Labour Government's defence policy. He travelled in the Far East, Africa and the Western hemisphere, bringing back and sending to the Foreign Office observations on the countries he had visited and assessments of their political leaders.

He found time for pleasure, too, regularly staying with Mr. Stavro Niarchos in the Aegean and the Mediterranean. When he shot with Niarchos in Spain, he was dressed not with his usual care but as untidily as most English country gentlemen who, out shooting, make no effort at all to rival Spanish graces. An important Spanish grandee went up to the Spanish Ambassador in London, the Marques de Santa Cruz, and asked disdainfully: "Who is that *secretario* with whom you have been conversing?"

Tony had other activities. Like all Lambtons up to his own generation he remained monogamous. He adored his children and he did not cease to care for Belinda. But he was fatally attractive to women. Wearing the dark glasses which his earlier eye troubles necessitated, he had a romantic, sensuous air and he stimulated excitement by his looks, his charm and his conversational gift. There is a touch of Lord Byron about Tony though he does not aspire to write poetry. He captivated some of the best-looking and most intelligent women in London society.

Early in 1970, Johnny Durham died and Tony succeeded him as 6th Earl of Durham, Viscount Lambton and, dating from Radical Jack's original peerage of 1828, Baron Durham.

Translation to the House of Lords would have interfered with a promising political career and so he took advantage of the Act of 1963 to disclaim his peerages. Strictly speaking this meant disclaiming all three of them; but he was well known in his constituency and elsewhere by the courtesy title of Viscount Lambton which he has held since 1941. So when a General Election was called in June, he stood as Viscount Lambton, the name familiar to his constituents. This caused a row in the House of Commons, and the Committee of Privileges, while admitting that courtesy titles had no relevance in law, ruled against him. However, the new Speaker, his old friend Selwyn Lloyd, declared in his favour on the perfectly sensible grounds that a courtesy title is, after all, only a courtesy title and carries no privileges or obligations. He had been briefly an earl and his children assumed and retained their courtesy titles, unlike Lord Home's children who dropped theirs. To most members of the House of Commons and to all the newspapers except the *Daily Telegraph*, which was purist, Tony remained Lord Lambton.

At the 1970 General Election he increased his majority at Berwick to over seven thousand and there was no doubt of his popularity in the constituency. The new Prime Minister, Ted Heath, whom, unlike Harold Macmillan, Tony respected and considered to have "a sense of purpose", appointed him Under Secretary of State at the Ministry of Defence, responsible for the Royal Air Force. The Minister of Defence was Lord Carrington, and Tony's responsibilities were not wholly comparable to those of the Secretary of State for Air before the service departments were amalgamated. Nevertheless, the assignment was an important one and his duties in the House and in a wider service area were far-reaching. It was an opportunity and a challenge.

Jaundice recurred in 1971 and again in 1972, and by the end of the latter year he was still feeling ill. This did not affect the conscientious exercise of his duties. He was, perhaps, a little diffident with the Air Marshals and inside the ministry, but his qualities were recognised and, as the

Labour M.P. Maurice Edelman subsequently wrote, "He had a sharp and independent mind, whose quality had long drawn the fire of the pompous and the envious."

On May 12th, 1973, Tony opened a debate in the House of Commons on the future of the Royal Air Force. His speech was generally approved on both sides of the House and there was little dissent from his proposals. He seemed to have his foot firmly placed on the ladder to higher preferment when, suddenly, the tocsin sounded.

As somebody once said, prostitutes and politics do not go well together. However, events have shown them to be closely allied. Since before Christmas 1972, Tony had been visiting an Irish call-girl by name of Norma Russell. She had recently married a self-confessed pimp called Colin Leavy who was a mini-cab driver in his spare time. Norma lived in some splendour in a flat in Maida Vale and had a number of affluent clients. At one time she even ran a thriving call-girl agency in the temporary absence of the lady who usually controlled it. Such an arrangement would have been well understood in Paris where the celebrated Madame Claude catered for rich Parisians and important foreign visitors. It was not likely to be so well understood in London. Colin Leavy for his part thought it might be financially advantageous if he took some compromising photographs and sold them to a newspaper.

The photographs, taken through a hole bored in a cupboard, were blurred and indistinct, and the *News of the World* to which Leavy and an accomplice offered them refused to buy. The paper did, however, at a comparatively low level and without editorial authority, make arrangements for a staff photographer to secure better ones on a future occasion. The *Sunday People*, to which the disconsolate Leavy and his friend went when rejected by the *News of the World*, paid them a few hundred pounds for the blurred originals.

By chance the police were engaged in a major anti-vice operation, largely concentrated on Soho. There they found a book containing Norma's address and they posted security agents outside her block of flats. On April 9th the Prime Minister learned that a member of the Government was involved, and a few days later he was told it was Lord Lambton. He took no action for over a month, because he heard there might also be criminal charges connected with drugs, charges which turned out to be false as far as Tony personally was concerned. Meanwhile, security agents posted outside another call-girl's flat discovered that Lord Jellicoe, Lord Privy Seal and Leader of the House of Lords, was an occasional visitor, though he had had no dealings with Norma.

This bomb exploded a year after Reginald Maudling, the Home Secretary, had been victimised for having quite innocently accepted the present of a silver coffee-pot from John Poulson, who later turned out to be the principal villain in a housing scandal; and only a week before, Heath, condemning large hand-outs by Mr. Tiny Rowlands' Lonrho, had spoken of the "unacceptable face of capitalism". Contemporaneous, and much more damaging to another "Establishment", was the Watergate scandal in the United States.

The newspaper photographs were not published, but were sent to Scotland Yard, a move which the papers concerned cited as proof of their responsible and law-abiding attitude. They did, however, print the story with glaring headlines and the popular press, which always finds it irresistible to stimulate public excitement in such cases, had a field-day. Tony's name was not at first mentioned, but he at once decided to make a full confession to the Prime Minister, to resign his office and to relinquish his seat in the House of Commons. Poor Lord Jellicoe was also caught in the net. He was one of the ablest ministers, with a first-class brain and considerable administrative experience; and he excelled as a speaker. He retired from politics and became in succession chairman of two great industrial companies whose shareholders were less censorious than the Houses of Parliament.

Meanwhile Norma caused a sensation by declaring, without any valid evidence, that a third minister was among her

171

clients. There are always rumours about Third Men, and sometimes Fourth and Fifth Men. Her statement hit the headlines, and the gossips in the clubs, the pubs and Fleet Street enjoyed themselves thoroughly. At one moment she declared there was a duke among her customers and several of those great noblemen, who had been a little wild in their youth, were actually offended when they heard that their names were only quoted at long odds. Norma herself thought it best to disappear, and so she and Colin Leavy went to Morocco, escorted and guarded by the *Sunday People*, until in July she decided to return to England and face the music, alleging that Colin had tried to murder her. Appearing in court she was fined £225. She later set up an establishment in Miami under a new name but was sentenced to deportation by the American immigration authorities.

Tony was shattered and utterly ashamed. All Lambtons, whatever their idiosyncrasies, have had a great regard for the truth and Tony made no attempt to excuse or minimise his offence. He declared that he had been incredibly stupid and knew that he had damaged the Government, the Conservative Party and his own family. Then and for many days afterwards he woke at 5 a.m. and lay in bed dreading what that morning's papers would print. One of the more fatuous newspaper comments was "To say the least it shows a lack of political judgment."

It is said of the newspapers that "Dog don't eat Dog". In this case the dogs devoured each other voraciously. The *Sunday Express* accused the *News of the World* of vicious behaviour and the *Daily Mail* entered the fray. The Managing Editor of the *Sunday Times* wrote in a letter to *The Times*: "Do the press have the right under some spurious moral pretext to do what the police cannot normally do without a warrant – enter a private house to photograph a citizen's private activities no matter which bed he may be in?" They abused each other with much more venom than they criticised Tony.

Two days after the news broke Tony did a courageous

thing. He gave a long interview on television to Robin Day in the course of which he admitted his folly and held nothing back. He apologised to his colleagues, to his constituents and to all who had trusted him. Though clearly racked by nervousness and emotion, he spoke with such sincerity that it was impossible not to be moved. Robin Day himself was scarcely less overcome, mainly because Tony insisted that his eleven-year-old son remain in the room during the transmission so as to listen to his father's confession.

The result was almost equally moving. Tony's Constituency Association begged him to remain their Member; both sides of the House of Commons applauded his courage, the frankness of his admissions and the dignity he had shown. The press almost unanimously followed suit. It was a tragedy that for a brief moment became almost a triumph. A Harris poll indicated that whereas sixty-three per cent of those questioned considered the Watergate scandal particularly serious, only twenty-four per cent thought that applied to the Lambton/Jellicoe affair. However, Tony said firmly: "I think it is quite inevitable that if you make a fool of yourself, and consequently embarrass the Government of which you are a Member, there is no alternative to resignation."

Needless to say a number of people, either for political reasons or because they were too stupid to realise that those who take prostitutes to bed do not, with their heads on the pillow, discuss guided weapons and electronic devices, raised the irrelevant security issue. George Wigg, prime prevaricator in the Profumo case and by now a peer, spoke in the House of Lords of the security risk and was even silly enough to suggest Tony might have given Norma advice about buying shares in the armaments industry. The *Sunday People*, anxious to justify itself in the face of violent attacks on its probity, declared that in this episode security was "a matter of urgent public concern". The Prime Minister prudently referred the matter to the Security Commission, sitting under Lord Diplock, which unanimously concluded that there was no breach of security at all. The Press Council, in its report, was a shade too unkind to the *News of the World* and not unkind enough to the *Sunday People*, which had actually paid the miscreants money.

There remained the criminal charge about drugs. Tony was neither a heavy drinker nor a drug addict. He admitted to having once smoked opium as an interesting experiment when travelling in the Far East, and he said he had also experimented with "pot" in Norma Leavy's flat. But drugs found in his house were mainly barbiturate pills, which the doctor had given him on prescription for his ills (and which Lord Moran had regularly prescribed for Winston Churchill) and partly a small amount of dried-up cannabis which had belonged to somebody else and which he had confiscated. All the same the cannabis was found in his room – or rather he voluntarily disclosed it to the police instead of destroying it – and the magistrates fined him £300.

Since the Second World War, scandals of a sexual kind have dogged the Conservative Party more than the Labour Party, though not every Labour M.P. has been as white as driven snow. Indeed, the political career of Tom Driberg, long a member of the Labour Party National Executive Committee, was only saved from extinction by a timely manoeuvre on the part of Lord Beaverbrook and his resourceful valet, Albert. Nor was he the sole Socialist sinner, though the Conservatives won by lengths in the Impurity Stakes.

The first prominent incident, which was exploited for purely political purposes, was the Profumo case. Nobody, least of all Jack Profumo himself, doubted that he had behaved reprehensibly, primarily because on a personal matter he told a lie to the House of Commons, a sin which is frequently committed by Members of Parliament, but usually only on political issues. He more than compensated for it by his singularly public-spirited activities afterwards, which won for him respect and approbation in all quarters and a decoration from the Queen.

Despite an allegation made by Lord Macaulay, the British public is not so ridiculous as to suffer from periodic fits of morality. On the contrary, like the American public, it thirsts for a scandal, especially one related to sex, and the media are always ready to oblige. What amplified the Profumo affair was the ruthless determination of certain leading figures on the Opposition benches to pretend a security risk was involved. This, as they well knew, was rubbish; but without giving a moment's thought to Profumo's distress, the front-bench moralists, such as Barbara Castle, who were wont to proclaim their monopoly of compassion, grasped the opportunity to discredit the Government, an exercise in which they were to a large extent successful. Another leader of the pack, George Wigg, was later arrested for kerb crawling, which may be taken as a commentary on the moral indignation he expressed.

There have been other sex scandals since the Lambton affair, in every case providing juicy headlines for the press and satisfaction for its readers. After the notorious affair relating to Cecil Parkinson and Miss Sara Keays, I sent this letter in verse to Charles Douglas-Home, the Editor of *The Times*:

Sir,
>
> Few of our island kith and kin
> Are totally immune to sin,
> Yet when some man the people know
> Is caught *flagrante delicto*,
> With feigned regret and hidden spite
> The sepulchres are painted white.
> Sometimes the plea's security;
> Sometimes it's national purity.
> Unleashing bloodhounds: splendid sport
> For those who've not themselves been caught.

In composing that letter, I was thinking of many other politicians who have become entangled in the barbed-wire fence erected by public prurience and political hypocrisy.

After the harrowing summer of 1973 Tony succumbed to an attack of jaundice even more severe than usual. It was another five years before a brilliant English doctor prescribed a remedy which cured him completely. Dissociating himself

175

from any form of politics he acquired a splendid sixteenth-century villa near Siena with a lovely garden. There he happily spends nine months of the year with a close and beautiful friend, in peace and comparative seclusion, devoting his renewed energies to writing books and short stories in an elegant style and usually with a touch of the macabre, of which *The Abbey in the Wood* is one of the more striking. They are much read and he finds literary endeavour, together with gardening, a serene contrast to the roughness of political life. His charm, hospitality and quick wit have retained old friendships and cemented new ones.

One of his daughters, Lucinda, has become an admired writer of books, a photographer and a skilful presenter of programmes on television. The success of these programmes has been enhanced by the originality and eccentricity of the subjects chosen, so that at least one family characteristic has been passed on to a later generation.

# Epilogue

The violent political storms which at intervals swept across the European continent from the time of the French Revolution to that of the Russian Revolution left Britain unscarred and seldom even shaken.

Several factors have contributed to the stability of Great Britain in the last three hundred years, a stability unique among the powerful and prominent nations of the Western world but unhappily one which stopped at the Irish Channel. The first and obvious factor is that even before the Reform Bill of 1832 there was in England, Scotland and Wales a framework of constitutional government that, whatever its blemishes, ensured a measure of freedom for the individual.

Secondly, although justice neither was nor is always delivered with an even hand, the rule of law was respected from the Glorious Revolution of 1688 onwards, a revolution far more significant for the development of constitutional government than either the French or American Revolutions a hundred years later. Even those like John Wilkes, whom the ruling caucus sought to persecute, could take refuge behind the solid bastions of the Common Law and the unmuzzled public opinion which supported it.

There was indeed a substantial element of freedom, but though all men were equal before the law (and in 1761 even an earl was hanged for murdering his land-steward), no obeisance at all was made to social equality. The conditions in which the poor lived, the tyranny to which workers and their children were subjected in mines, factories and "dark satanic mills", the harsh discipline inflicted on soldiers and sailors, the cruelty in schools, are all familiar horrors. As portrayed by Charles Dickens, they are said to have been long presented in the Soviet Union as an accurate picture of life in the British Isles today.

In the last seventy years of nineteenth-century Britain strenuous efforts were made to improve matters. The Factory Acts and Poor Law Reform extracted quite a lot of stings before the wounds festered, as did the legalising of trade unions; and despite the sweated labour prevalent when the Industrial Revolution was at its insensitive zenith, and even as late as the beginning of the twentieth century, there was no shortage of beneficent societies and individuals to counteract at least some of the miseries of urban penury. Through church schools and ragged schools many children of the poor were given a smattering of education. Religious organisations devoted to helping the derelict and the destitute sprang into life. By twentieth-century standards the efforts made were inadequate: by nineteenth-century standards, and by comparison with most foreign lands, they were humane, widespread and a source of somewhat smug national gratification.

No less responsible for Britain's, as opposed to Ireland's, social quiescence was the attitude of many of the "haves" to the "have-nots". Whereas in Ireland the big estates often belonged to absentees, distanced by race and religion from the peasantry, in England there were no peasants living in wretched hovels of mud and straw. It is true that, unlike Radical Jack, the owners of coal mines, who were usually also great landowners, tended to be ignorant of industrial matters and inattentive to their responsibilities. But as agricultural landlords they mostly wore another face. They provided cottages for their agricultural labourers, more often than not knew them personally, talked to them without apparent condescension and paid attention to their welfare. So did their wives and children, however grand they might be in a wider society.

There were, of course, exceptions and there were arrogant idlers; but the majority of British aristocrats, unlike their French equivalent, lived on the land, were impartial Justices of the Peace (except with regard to poachers), sent their younger sons into the army, the navy or the Church, and took an active part in the administration of counties, country towns and villages. They were a powerful element in the legislature, but they were also the local constitutional monarchs.

The agricultural workers were poorly paid, as were the hordes of domestic servants, but they were seldom unkindly treated and, Tolpuddle Martyrs or not, their simple livelihood was usually secure. A labourer's own vegetable garden and free milk for his children were normal perquisites, so was wood for the fire and sometimes a sack of coal. In times of distress, *noblesse oblige* meant the reduction or total remission of farm-rents. Doubtless the labourers seldom besought the Almighty to bless the squire and his relations; but they do not seem to have borne envy, whatever the other deadly sins in which they indulged. Probably because they were so little educated, and so deprived of yardsticks by which to make comparisons, they were no more discontented with their lot than human beings, rich or poor, normally are. They were less so than many of their descendants who watch television and live in greater affluence.

Envy only rose to the top of the list of the seven deadly sins when comparisons became readily available.

Those who think that this is too rosy a picture of nineteenth-century British society must still account for the fact that the turbulent revolutionary gales of 1830, 1848 and 1870 scarcely rustled in Britain. The breeze of public discontent was a comparatively gentle one, mainly confined to the 1830s and 1840s when the Chartist Movement prospered briefly until it withered pathetically into a petition delivered to Parliament, like William IV's crown, in a Hackney carriage. Britain's insularity contributed to stability, but though the English Channel saved the island from military invasion, it was not a barrier to the interflow of ideas.

Mercantile and industrial supremacy resulted in the still firmer entrenchment of a middle class which had thrived in London since Plantagenet times. Thence came the innovation in science and engineering, the political philosophers, the painters and the novelists, though seldom the patrons and purchasers of works of art. The French, as well as the German and Italian kingdoms and grand duchies, had their *bourgeoisie* too; but neither they, nor even the Swiss and the Dutch, matched the British middle class in numbers, wealth and inventiveness. This increasingly prosperous segment of society is generally believed to have been the bulwark against revolution. In fact, although many of its members were liberal, generous and benevolent, it was also from this source that the harsh industrial task-masters and the colonial slave-owners came. Liberalism and the persuasive influence of moderation stemmed at least as much from the upper as from the middle classes: perhaps more so, for the upper classes were predominant in both Houses of Parliament.

A fair measure of the credit for the smoothness of change in the British Isles belongs to those members of the landed aristocracy who put themselves in the forefront of innovation. Many of the powerful landowners, such as Grey and Shaftesbury, Althorp and Rosebery, were active reformers, but none were more ardently so than the vastly rich and locally dominant John George Lambton. Radical Jack was not the revolutionary zealot that many of his contemporaries asserted him to be; but he certainly was one of the most prominent founding fathers of long overdue parliamentary reform.

Equally important, the British Empire was a plant which he saved from withering in the face of indifference and hostility, though it flowered and grew to vast proportions after he himself was dead. Conquest and commerce established the empire; statesmanship enabled it to evolve, largely unruffled, until such time as it reached maturity and transformed itself into a Commonwealth united only by tradition and sentiment.

Durham must often have seemed insufferable to his contemporaries. That is not unusual in great men and women especially when they are, as great men and women tend to be, far-sighted, imaginative and intolerant of those slower-witted than themselves. If he gave cause for dislike, he was also held in awe. While he was on his way home from Canada, Melbourne wrote to a colleague: "It is very odd to see this terror that Durham inspires. Everybody has always been afraid of him."

The British aristocracy was never a closed caste, like those on the continent of Europe, and throughout the centuries there were always infusions of new blood. All the same, the eldest sons of peers did usually marry into other great families, frequently by a *mariage de convenance* which more often than not brought contentment, if not necessarily fidelity. Their descendants have flung their matrimonial net (and frequently nets) into distant and sometimes stormy waters. Divorce is no longer thought reprehensible, let alone socially ostracised. The broken home is acceptable to all but the children it victimises. Vulgarity and hedonism are more fashionable than dignity and dedication. The rules by which aristocratic society once judged its members apply no more and there is now only a trickle of "blue blood", concentrated in a score or so of ancient families and diminishing rapidly. The noblemen have fled the field of politics to concentrate on realising their endangered assets, to insert their names in the *Dictionary of Directors*, to enjoy field sports, relax in foreign lands or even just spend their money in smart restaurants and night-clubs.

The famous names which up till the Second World War, and for some thirty years after it, were prominent in every ministerial list are no longer seen; for most of the younger generation have had neither the incentive nor the talent to follow on. There are exceptions, but the abdication has been almost wholesale. The Conservative Party is now the domain of a diligent, enterprising and aggressive middle class, and the Liberal grandees became an extinct species after Lloyd George succeeded Asquith as Prime Minister in the First World War.

Radical Jack founded a dynasty which had blood as blue as the grotto in Capri. Since his day it has displayed eccentricity, but not degeneracy. His children and grandchildren made no achievements as lasting as his own, though in a variety of forms they inherited his kaleidoscopic characteristics; but a later generation do appear to have inherited some of his gifts. Now that ardent, ambitious professionals have filled the vacant stalls, it will be surprising if ever again a Lambton, or a scion of any of the other great landowning families whose names were recently so familiar feels it is his or her inherited duty to seek the political power their predecessors coveted and often attained. There may be exceptions, but they are rare.

In the reign of King James I Sir Randolph Crewe, Lord Chief Justice of England, speaking of the extinction of the De Vere family and the ancient earldom of Oxford, said this:

Time hath his revolution. There must be a period and an end of all temporal things, *finis rerum*, an end of names and dignities and whatsoever is terrene; and why not of De Vere? For where is Bohun? Where is Mowbray? Where is Mortimer? Nay, which is more and most of all, where is Plantagenet? They are entombed in the urns and sepulchres of mortality.

So, politically and in due course territorially, must it be for the families which inherited the traditions and opportunities that had been De Vere's. Those whose forbears showed an adaptability to changing circumstances which made them immune to revolutions raging in other lands, cannot escape the revolution of time.

# Envoi

Anybody who has ever met Tony Lambton will know that he has a tendency to mumble.

After my father died in November, 1987, Tony ordered a wreath from a London florist. When he arrived to collect it on his way to the funeral, he was horrified to find a monstrosity. "Two metres by two metres was *definitely* what you ordered," the lady said firmly.

"Two feet by two feet," he protested lamely.

Too big to fit in his car, and in any case only suitable for the funeral of the likes of Al Capone, he was forced to leave the wreath and a large cheque behind.

At a particularly sad time for all of us – my mother, brother, sister and myself – we all had a good laugh at Tony's misfortune.

My father would have laughed too.

Sandy Colville
December 21, 1987

# Index